THEY THINK
IT'S ALL SHITE
...It Is Now!

THEY THINK IT'S ALL SHITE

...It Is Nw!

An Alternative Guide
to the World Cup

A. PARODY

Michael O'Mara Books Limited

First published in Great Britain in 2006 by
Michael O'Mara Books Limited
9 Lion Yard
Tremadoc Road
London SW4 7NQ

A CIP catalogue record for this book is available from the British Library

ISBN (10 digit): 1-84317-210-0
ISBN (13 digit): 978-1-84317-210-9

1 3 5 7 9 10 8 6 4 2

Designed and typeset by E-Type

Printed and bound in Great Britain by Cox & Wyman, Reading, Berks

Photograph Acknowledgements

Daniel Motz/Empics – 9; Peter Robinson/Empics – 12, 92, 95;
Tony Marshall/Empics – 15; DPA/Empics – 17; Central Press/
Getty Images – 20; S&G/Empics/Alpha – 23, 27; PA/Empics – 35;
Evening Standard/Getty Images – 40; Sydney O'Meara/*Evening
Standard*/Getty Images – 43; Neal Simpson/Empics – 46, 126;
PA Photos/ABACA/Empics – 53; *Lancashire Evening Post* – 58, 148;
Getty Images – 66, 79, 93, 100, 120, 135, 140; Ross Kinnaird/
Empics – 69; PA Photos/DPA/Empics – 76; Bongarts/Getty Images
– 85; AFP/Getty Images – 107, 113, 129, 144;
Martina Hellmann/Empics/DPA – 158.

CONTENTS

INTRODUCTION

Bigger even than the LDV Vans Trophy, the World Cup is soccer's showpiece event. The world's greatest footballers gather every four years for a festival of fair play where sportsmanship is king. Referees' decisions are never disputed, players make no attempt to gain an unfair advantage over their opponents by cheating in any shape or form, and losing is always done with good grace. And it's all played out against a carnival-like backdrop with fans of rival nations happily sitting side-by-side under one roof, exchanging pleasantries and amusing anecdotes while the local police smile benevolently. Well, that's what it probably says in the FIFA brochure. But like a half-finished Spanish hotel block, the truth is less concrete. For the stakes are so high that the World Cup has become riddled with all the things that are bad about football – rioting, cheating, dissent, foul play, official team songs and, perhaps worst of all, Ian Wright in the BBC studio.

Here we unashamedly chronicle seventy-six years of inglorious World Cup history – the scandals and embarrassments, the bust-ups and cock-ups. So forget the hype, this is all about the *real* World Cup.

Antal Parody
March 2006

CHEATS SOMETIMES PROSPER

THE HAND OF GOD

These days Sir Bobby Robson is viewed as a venerable elder statesman of the game, a man of wisdom and dignity, but also with the charm of a lovable uncle in the first stages of Alzheimer's. His ability for getting players' names wrong has become legendary. When Shola Ameobi teamed up with the England Under-21 side, their then manager David Platt asked him what his nickname was. Ameobi said he hadn't got one. 'Well,' persisted Platt, 'what does Bobby Robson call you at Newcastle?' 'Carl Cort,' replied Ameobi.

But Robson has not always been held in such affection. The role of England manager inevitably carries a government health warning. As a job, it presents an even greater challenge than that of John McCririck's tailor. And by the 1986 World Cup, Robson was coming under regular tabloid fire for his apparent indecision over matters of team selection and tactics. England's path to the finals in Mexico was tinged with controversy, particularly with the Romanians accusing them of not trying against Northern Ireland, who thus qualified at Romania's expense. Meanwhile, Bryan Robson's shoulder seemed to be held in place by little more than Sellotape, and when he dislocated it again – during a feeble goalless draw with Morocco in the second group game in Mexico – 'Captain Marvel' was about as much use to the team as Captain Birds Eye. In the same match, Ray Wilkins was sent off for throwing the ball at the Paraguayan referee, which was totally out of character as Wilkins had never previously been known to move the ball in a forward direction. Almost by default, Bobby Robson now stumbled on a winning team. The mysteriously discarded Peter Beardsley was recalled and, with Gary Lineker as his Esmerelda, formed a union that captured the nation's hearts and destroyed first Poland and then Paraguay to set up a quarter-final meeting with Argentina – the first clash between the two countries since the Falklands War.

With both governments pleading 'Don't mention the war', manager Robson set about devising a cunning plan to thwart the genius of Argentina's star player, Diego Maradona. Kneecapping him, handing him a signed photo of Beardsley before kick-off, getting each England player in turn to tell him that his bootlaces were undone – these ideas were all discarded in favour of instructing Terry Butcher and Terry Fenwick not to tackle the little maestro. It was an order they carried out to perfection in the fifty-sixth minute as Maradona waltzed through the entire England defence to put Argentina 2–0 up. But by then, England were in a state of shock, still reeling from the events of four minutes earlier, when Steve Hodge had sliced an attempted

Like Joe Bugner in his prime, Shilton was easily beaten to the punch.

clearance towards his own goal, and, with Peter Shilton slow to come off his line, Maradona had nipped in and palmed the ball into the net. Shilton, showing quicker reactions than he had for the goal, immediately appealed for handball but the Tunisian referee, Ali Bennaceur, ignored the protest. Later, the hapless Bennaceur prevented a possible England goal by standing on the end of the Argentine wall at a free kick. Robson brought on John Barnes, who had recently spent a happy night in Rio (something that one or two Premiership players probably fantasize about), but although Lineker managed to pull one goal back, understandably there were dark mutterings in the dressing room after the game.

For his part, Maradona was innocence personified. When Terry Butcher asked him whether he had handled the ball, the cheeky Argentine maestro smiled and pointed to his head. By mastering two actions at the same time, Maradona instantly put himself on a different plane to Butcher. Maradona subsequently conceded that if a hand had been involved, it must have been the Hand of God.

Maradona's cheating enabled Bobby Robson to play the victim, shaking his head mournfully at the first sight of a notepad. Instead of calling for his resignation, many journalists actually began to feel sorry for him. Just as an untimely death can revive a fading music career, the Hand of God goal turned out to be a good career move for the wronged Robson, who thereafter

SHITE FACT

At the 1986 finals, during the games against Morocco and Paraguay, England fielded two defenders by the name of Gary Stevens – one who played for Spurs, the other for Everton. This led to the England fans chanting: 'Two Gary Stevens . . . there's only two Gary Stevens.'

adopted a Joan of Arc persona – or Noah of Arc as he would have doubtless put it. Bookmakers William Hill were equally outraged and offered to refund all stake money to any of their customers who had bet on a draw, claiming that 'the moral result should have been 1–1.' When bookmakers start talking about refunds and morality, it's a clear indication of the seriousness of the crime committed by Maradona against the English nation at the 1986 World Cup.

ARGENTINA IN A FIX?

Argentina were surely destined to win the 1978 World Cup. Not only did they have some excellent players and a charismatic coach in César Luis Menotti (who was to cigarettes what Sir Alex Ferguson is to gum), but they were also the home nation and seemed to experience a touch of divine intervention on the way to the final, which left a suspicion that even if some matches in the tournament were not actually bent, they were at the very least a little curved. Opposition coaches had been concerned from the outset that referees would favour Argentina, and the performance of Portuguese official António Garrido, who awarded the hosts a penalty and sent off two Hungarians in Argentina's first game, did little to dispel those fears. In their second match, referee Jean Dubach of Switzerland gifted Argentina a penalty before refusing a far more blatant one for the French. Swedish referee Ulf Eriksson was next to fuel the conspiracy theories during the second-round match with Poland. Having awarded the Poles a clear-cut penalty, he insisted on repositioning the ball just as Kazimierz Deyna was about to take the kick. Deyna, in his 100th international, duly missed and Argentina went on to win 2–0.

Yet these examples were mere trifling irritations compared with what was to come. After each team had played two matches in the second-round groups, Brazil and Argentina were level on points at the top of Group B with Brazil having a superior goal

Peru keeper Ramón Quiroga describes the one that got away.
Otherwise it would have been 7–0.

difference of one. Brazil had to play Poland in their final game and Argentina faced Peru, who were already certain of being eliminated from the competition. Brazil were due to kick off in the afternoon, but Argentina were not playing until the evening, which meant that they would know exactly what they had to do (and how many goals they needed to score) in order to progress to the final. Delia Smith could not have come up with a better recipe for disaster. Brazil protested at the unfairness of the schedule, but their pleas inevitably fell on deaf ears. Brazil beat Poland 3–1, leaving Argentina needing to win by four clear goals to reach the final. Peru elected to field a weakened team, which included four inexperienced reserves, and, despite having conceded only six goals in their previous five games, the Peruvian side meekly surrendered 6–0. So vehement were the accusations levelled at Peru's eccentric goalkeeper Ramón Quiroga (who just happened to have been born in Argentina) that he felt obliged to write an open letter defending himself. As allegations of bribery became rife, it was revealed that the Argentina Central Bank had, at around the time of the crucial match, suddenly decided to unfreeze $50 million in credit for Peru. And shortly after the tournament, Argentina shipped 35,000 tonnes of free grain to Peru as a 'humanitarian gesture'. The timing in both cases was explained away as pure coincidence.

Given their track record, it came as no surprise when the Argentines objected to FIFA's appointed referee for the final – the firm Israeli Abraham Klein, who had overseen Argentina's 1–0 defeat to Italy in their third group game. Instead the Argentine camp managed to persuade FIFA to replace Klein with Italy's Sergio Gonella, whose performance comfortably maintained the dismal standard of officialdom at the tournament.

So was Argentina's game with Peru fixed? We all know there's only one man who could have fixed it properly . . . but Jimmy Savile was a busy man back in 1978.

SHITE FACT

Mexican fans were so incensed by their team's defensive tactics in gaining the 0–0 draw necessary to qualify for the 1990 finals that they took to cheering the visiting United States players instead.

FLARE-UP IN RIO

There is so much cheating in modern life. People cheat on their partners, they cheat on the golf course and they cheat at the supermarket by hiding a pack of honey-roast ham beneath their frozen cod steaks so that they can sneak seven items through the 'six items or less' checkout.

Arguably the most flagrant episode of cheating in the World Cup took place at the Maracanã Stadium, Rio de Janeiro, during a crucial qualifying match in September 1989. Chile were trailing 1–0 to Brazil when a flare was thrown on to the pitch. Chile's captain and goalkeeper Roberto Rojas immediately collapsed as if he had been hit by the flare and was carried off on a stretcher, bleeding copiously from the wound. Apparently fearing for their own safety, his teammates refused to stay on the pitch to finish the game, and so the match was abandoned. Then it emerged that Rojas had been feigning the injury and had cut himself deliberately with a razor blade in the hope that Chile would be awarded the tie. In fact the flare had landed some way from the keeper, and the blood had only appeared *after* the arrival of the Chilean trainer. In the light of the new evidence, Brazil were now awarded the win, Rojas was banned for life and Chile were barred from competing in the 1994 World Cup. Six more members of the Chilean entourage – including the Federation President, the team doctor (who had issued a fake medical certificate), the kit man and the physiotherapist – also received bans. Ironically the one person who profited from the shameful charade was the woman who threw the flare, Rosemary de Mello. Lapping up her fifteen minutes of fame, presumably with the help of a Brazilian version of Max Clifford, she went on to appear in *Playboy* magazine. Well, the Brazilians always have admired a woman with flare . . .

SHITE FACT

In their 1930 semi-final with Yugoslavia, hosts Uruguay scored their third goal after the ball went out of play and was kicked back on by a uniformed policeman. The match officials wisely chose to look the other way. Uruguay won 6–1.

AND THE WINNER IS . . .

The time will surely come when the actual games of football played at the World Cup are of secondary importance. Instead the real interest will surround the awards night when a glittering array of celebrities gather to recognize the tournament's outstanding achievers in such categories as Best Spitter, Best Hairstyle, Most Innovative Way of Winning a Penalty, Most Colourful Language at a Match Official, and of course the Stan Collymore Award for Best Dogging. Naturally there would also be a Best Simulation Award to acknowledge the rising art of play-acting and if such a category had been in place at the 2002 World Cup finals, there could only have been one possible winner . . . Rivaldo.

It was Rivaldo's one-man show in the Group C game with Turkey that proved that although some of his teammates'

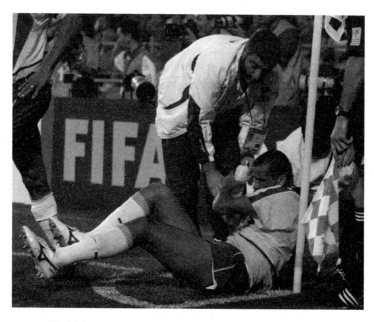

Rivaldo's only regret was not incorporating a double pike and twist into his back flip.

acting skills could only match those of an extra in *Neighbours*, Rivaldo's abilities were clearly on a par with the great Lord Olivier. As he prepared to take a last-minute corner with Brazil leading 2–1, Rivaldo took centre stage. Impatient and frustrated, Turkish midfielder Hakan Ünsal kicked the ball at the Barcelona player – an unwise gesture, particularly as he had already been booked. Although the ball hit him on the legs, Rivaldo immediately fell backwards to the ground clutching his face in apparent agony. Either he was a poor judge of anatomy or, as the head of Turkey's football association suggested icily, he was having a brain haemorrhage. The Korean referee Kim Young Joo promptly sent the Turk off, but when the incident was replayed on the giant screen at the Ulsan Stadium, a chorus of boos echoed around the ground.

Rivaldo tried to defend his theatrics, saying, 'I think he deserved to be sent off. You don't do the sort of thing he did, so he deserved the sending-off. Of course he didn't get me in a place where I could be hurt, but I used my experience.' His coach, 'Big Phil' Scolari, mounted an equally feeble defence, with the bizarre claim that 'Rivaldo made a defensive movement because the ball hit him on the leg and was travelling upwards.' But neither explanation cut any ice with FIFA who fined the former World Player of the Year £4,500 for his dying swan routine.

SHITE FACT

After losing 1–0 to unfancied North Korea and thus crashing out of the 1966 World Cup, the Italian team dreaded the journey home. In a bid to escape their fans' fury they even switched flight destinations, but were still unable to avoid being pelted with rotten tomatoes on arrival at Genoa airport.

A PAIN IN SPAIN

Traditionally, the Germans are more dangerous than Dick Cheney on a hunting vacation, so when they began their campaign in España '82 by sensationally falling 2–1 to unfancied Algeria, the result sent shock waves around the footballing world. Although normal service was resumed with a 4–1 victory over Chile, West Germany's passage to the second round rested on the outcome of their final group match with Austria. The Austrians meanwhile had won their opening two games, which meant that by the time they faced West Germany in Gijón, both countries knew that they would progress at the expense of Algeria (who had played and won the previous day) if the Germans were allowed a narrow victory. A draw or a win for Austria would see Germany eliminated, and a German victory by three goals or more would knock out Austria. But 1–0 to the Germans, that would do nicely. Thus the neighbours

After both sides progressed conveniently to the next round, the West German and Austrian players embarked on a display of congratulatory back-slapping (or should that be back-scratching?).

made a secret pact whereby, after Horst Hrubesch had given the Germans an early lead, the match was allowed to drift aimlessly to a conclusion. As a spectacle, it was about as exciting as a match summary by Tony Adams. Predictably, the aggrieved Algerians protested at the fiasco, but, equally predictably, FIFA did nothing.

It was not the first time the Germans had been accused of exploiting the World Cup rules. For the 1954 competition in Switzerland, the sixteen finalists were divided into four groups. Two teams were seeded in each group, and, bizarrely, they played only the weakest countries in the first round, the aim being to reduce the number of shock results. It was probably the worst idea since King Alfred decided to leave the cakes in for just a little bit longer. West Germany and South Korea were drawn in the same group as seeded teams Hungary and Turkey. That Turkey were seeded at all was something of a mystery, their standing in world football at the time being slightly below that of Corinthian Casuals. But the organizers in their wisdom had determined the seeded teams even before the qualifying tournament began, so that when Turkey ousted one of the seeds, Spain (by virtue of lots drawn from a hat by a blindfolded Italian boy), they automatically assumed the Spaniards' seeded status. The folly of making Turkey one of the tournament favourites was quickly exposed when the West Germans hammered them 4–1 in their opening group game. Meanwhile, Hungary put nine past South Korea. It was then that the West German manager, Sepp Herberger, started to plan ahead.

SHITE FACT

A Uruguayan car salesman offered to reimburse recent customers in full if Uruguay won the 2002 World Cup. If they only got through the first round, he said he would knock 10 per cent off the purchase price. As it was they fell at the first hurdle, meaning that he didn't have to hand back a single peso.

Convinced that his team could defeat Turkey in a play-off, should the two countries finish level on points, Herberger deliberately fielded a weakened side against Hungary in the hope of avoiding Brazil in the quarter-finals. Sure enough, Hungary crushed the depleted Germans 8–3, and with Turkey scoring seven against the hapless South Koreans, the runners-up spot had to be decided by a play-off in which, parading a revitalized, full-strength line-up, West Germany hammered Turkey 7–2. This left group winners Hungary to face mighty Brazil, while the Germans faced considerably less daunting opposition in the form of Yugoslavia. As it panned out, Hungary and West Germany met again in the final. Just two weeks after being humbled 8–3, the Germans, with all their rested or injured players miraculously recovered, turned the tables to win 3–2 and lift the World Cup. But the sweet smell of success had been tarnished by more than a faint whiff of gamesmanship.

1966 AND ALL THAT

In common with other nationalities, the English are adept at rewriting history to suit their own ends. Just as the Italians prefer to forget Mussolini and many Germans refuse to acknowledge the very existence of Kraftwerk, so the English tend to gloss over any contentious issues surrounding their 1966 World Cup triumph. But allegations of home bias were almost as loud then as they were in Argentina in 1978 and South Korea in 2002. En route to the semi-final, England had played every game at their beloved Wembley, but it was expected that the semi against Portugal would be played at Goodison Park instead. So when it was finally announced that the match would take place at Wembley after all, there were mutterings of discontent about favouritism from many foreign observers.

And when it came to the final, there are question marks about all three of Geoff Hurst's goals. The free kick that led to the first was taken while Swiss referee Gottfried Dienst was lecturing a

Geoff Hurst was declared the winner of this 1966 Spot the Ball competition.

German player; the second hit the bar and bounced down so quickly that Dienst had to consult his Azerbaijani colleague Tofik Bahkramov (who later became known as 'the Russian linesman'), who duly awarded the goal even though he was poorly positioned some ten yards from the goal line; and the third was scored at a time when three spectators had run on to the pitch. Of course the most controversial of these was Hurst's second (England's third). Although subsequent freeze-frame analysis has failed to prove that the whole of the ball crossed the line, England fans have insisted that it must have been a goal because Roger Hunt turned away to celebrate rather than knock the ball into the net. But this is Roger Hunt they're talking about. Because he had already run more than five yards to get into that position, he had therefore reached the peak of his physical limits. He didn't stop because he thought it was a goal – he later admitted that he wouldn't have reached the ball anyway; no, he was turning round because he was like the bunny in the Duracell adverts whose batteries were about to run out.

Thus the England fan is left on the horns of a dilemma. On the one hand, strictly in the sense of fair play and sportsmanship on which we were all raised, we should acknowledge that in the absence of any conclusive evidence that the entire ball crossed the line, the historic victory was, to say the least, dubious. On the other hand, it was against the Germans, so who cares?

SHITE FACT

Plans to produce a special World Cup stamp depicting the sixteen nations taking part in the 1966 finals were scrapped on the orders of the Foreign Office because the British government did not officially recognize North Korea. So the design of the stamps was hastily changed and the Royal Mail promises they should be delivered any day now . . .

MONUMENTAL BALLS-UPS

SELECTION HEADACHE

You know what it's like with builders: they can never finish a job. Look at the Temple of Zeus in Athens – they went off for a tea break in 510 BC and didn't come back for another 700 years. Rumour has it that the same firm won the contract to build the new Wembley Stadium. It was much the same story at the 1950 World Cup, where the Maracanã Stadium in Rio de Janeiro had still not been completed by the time the tournament began. This didn't present too much of a problem until a deciding group match between Yugoslavia and Brazil in July. Shortly before kick-off, Yugoslavia's influential forward Rajko Mitic stood up in the dressing room and banged his head on a protruding iron girder. Forced to take the field without him, the Yugoslavs went through the formality of being introduced to the Mayor of Rio but then headed straight back to the dressing room, hotly pursued by referee Mervyn Griffiths of Wales. With Griffiths refusing to delay the kick-off while Mitic received treatment, Yugoslavia had to

SHITE FACT

The kick-off for the 1974 final between West Germany and Holland was delayed when English referee Jack Taylor spotted that the groundstaff had forgotten to position any corner flags on the Munich pitch.

start the game a man short and promptly went a goal down inside three minutes. Mitic – his head heavily bandaged – was eventually able to join the action, but the damage had been done and Yugoslavia slipped out of the tournament 2–0.

A TALE OF TWO KEVINS

The 1973 World Cup qualifier between England and Poland at Wembley will always be remembered for the unorthodox but ultimately highly effective goalkeeping of Jan Tomaszewski, the man famously derided by Brian Clough as a 'clown'. But it was also the scene of a hilarious piece of slapstick on the bench involving England substitutes Kevin Keegan and Kevin Hector. With just five minutes remaining and England needing another goal to qualify, Sir Alf Ramsey belatedly decided to send on Kevin Hector. 'Kevin, get stripped,' he barked. Thinking Ramsey meant him, Kevin Keegan started getting changed instead,

England's failure to go for the juggler left them thwarted by the 'clown'.

reserve goalkeeper Ray Clemence even helping Keegan to take off his tracksuit in order to speed up the operation. Only then did Ramsey, realizing he was about to send on the wrong Kevin, clarify his instructions. By the time Kevin Hector did get on to the pitch there were only ninety seconds left. It was all too late; the 1–1 scoreline marking the end of England's World Cup '74 qualifying campaign. So the Poles and their 'clown' went through to the finals. And ironically it was Clough who years later would end up with the red nose.

HE SAID WHAT?

'I've never seen a bloke play so badly and so great inside one match.'

Pat Jennings sums up Polish goalkeeper Jan Tomaszewski's performance at Wembley in 1973

PANTOMIME ORSI

Italy's equalizer in their 2–1 victory over Czechoslovakia in the 1934 final came courtesy of a remarkable shot by their Argentine winger Raimundo Orsi, who conjured up a strike that dipped and swerved at the last minute to leave Czech keeper Frantisek Plánicka utterly bamboozled. When a few scribes had the temerity to suggest to Orsi that his goal was a fluke, the little chap bridled and demanded the opportunity to prove himself. So the day after the final, Orsi returned to the stadium in Rome to show a battery of journalists and photographers exactly how he did it. Without even a goalkeeper to beat, twenty times he tried to recreate his famous shot and twenty times he failed miserably. Eventually, with no hint of a swerve or a dip on the horizon, he gave up in disgust and went home.

SHITE FACT

In 1996, city authorities in Verona who planned to name a new stadium in memory of Italy's 1938 World Cup winning goalkeeper Aldo Olivieri scrapped the idea after discovering that he was still alive and well at the grand old age of eighty-five.

SUPREME EMBARRASSMENT

It must have seemed like a good idea at the time: as the climax to the opening ceremony for the 1994 finals, the American organizers would arrange for a world-famous entertainer to take a symbolic penalty kick. If they had chosen Rod Stewart, Jon Bon Jovi – even Stevie Wonder – it might have worked, but instead they picked Diana Ross. Let's be honest, Diana Ross would have struggled to make a Motown XI (Gladys Knight would surely have pipped her), and although her red trouser-suit and poodle perm were eerily reminiscent of Kevin Keegan in his Liverpool days, she scarcely looked the part as she tottered up to the spot. In her favour was the fact that nothing, apparently, had been left to chance. The ball had been placed just a few yards from the goal and the keeper had been instructed to dive out of the way. Alas, in front of a crowd of 63,000 inside Chicago's Soldier Field Stadium and a worldwide television audience of millions, Miss Ross screwed the ball hopelessly wide. Suddenly Geoff Thomas's infamous Wembley strike didn't look half so bad. AIN'T NO GOALPOSTS WIDE ENOUGH screamed the headlines as Miss Ross returned to her day job. Nor was she the only celebrity casualty during that calamitous opening ceremony: singer Jon Secada had to deliver the US national anthem with only his head and shoulders visible after falling through a hole in the stage and dislocating his shoulder; while talk-show queen Oprah Winfrey fell flat on her face as she climbed down from the stage. But these were mere supporting acts to the glory that was Diana. And when, a month later, Italy's Roberto Baggio ('the Divine Ponytail') blazed a penalty over the bar to hand the World Cup to Brazil, the tournament achieved a neat symmetry – beginning and ending with a dreadful penalty miss by a star with a lousy hairstyle.

SHITE FACT

Ten Scotland fans following their side in Bordeaux for the 1998 World Cup spent £600 on a takeaway order of lager and curry, which they telephoned through to an Indian restaurant in Bournemouth. They then spent another £800 on a charter flight to deliver it to Bordeaux.

TRAINER'S OWN GOAL

The 1930 semi-final between Argentina and the United States (which Argentina won 6–1) was notable for the untimely intervention of the US team trainer Jack Coll. Still raging over a disputed Argentine goal, Coll ran on to the pitch to treat an injured player. In a visible display of temper, he threw down his medical bag, broke a bottle of chloroform and accidentally anaesthetized himself, as a result of which he had to be carried off by his own team.

FA IN A PICKLE

The Jules Rimet Trophy was the jewel in football's crown – a piece of silverware insured for the princely sum of £30,000. So what did the Football Association do when entrusted with its

In 1966 it was Pickles' preserve to get the FA out of a jam.

care and safety prior to the 1966 finals? They put it on display at a public stamp exhibition in Central Hall, Westminster, where security was so lax that a stick of Right Guard would have offered greater protection. Perhaps realizing that they would probably have been better off handing the precious trophy over to the Kray twins, FIFA were initially reluctant to let it out of their sight, but were won over by the FA's assurance that it would be guarded round the clock (by Laurel and Hardy). Sure enough, the trophy had only been on display for forty-eight hours when the guards returned from a break to discover that it had vanished. Cue much scratching of heads and an embarrassed array of red faces.

Scotland Yard's finest were immediately put on the case, but it took a mongrel dog called Pickles to rescue the situation a week later. David Corbett was walking Pickles in Norwood, South London, when the dog began sniffing around a brown paper bundle hidden under a garden hedge. Inside was the World Cup. While Corbett was financially rewarded, Pickles became an overnight celebrity and was honoured with an invitation to the celebration banquet that followed England's victory in the final. Given that Pickles had salvaged the FA's reputation, the banquet should really have been held under his rules. Surely it wouldn't have been too much of a hardship for

SHITE FACT

After scoring the penalty in the 2–1 defeat of Brazil that earned Italy a place in the 1938 final, 'Peppino' Meazza felt his shorts, which had already been torn earlier in the game, slip down around his ankles. Luckily his quick-thinking teammates crowded around him to spare his blushes until a new pair were brought out.

SHITE FACT

To prevent the World Cup trophy from falling into the hands of the Nazis, FIFA's Italian Vice-President Dr Ottorino Barassi kept it hidden in a shoe box under his bed throughout the Second World War.

men in high office to wear studded dog collars and crawl around on all fours?

ONE TEAM IN TALLINN, THERE'S ONLY ONE TEAM IN TALLINN

The Scottish football team usually travels about as well as parsnip wine but, having won 2–0 in Latvia four days previously, they were quietly confident of picking up three more points from their qualifying game against Estonia in October 1996. However, when manager Craig Brown saw how low the temporary floodlights in Tallinn's Kadriorg Stadium were positioned, he was worried that they would dazzle his goalkeeper. This was clearly a cause for concern because usually it takes only the ball to dazzle a Scottish goalkeeper. Scotland duly protested to FIFA who, on the morning of the match, ordered the kick-off to be brought forward from 6.45 p.m. to 3 p.m. But Estonian officials were irked by this slight on their technology and had no intention of complying. So when the Scottish team and the match officials walked onto the pitch shortly before 3 p.m., they did so in splendid isolation. For the Estonia team were still finishing off their lunch in a hotel fifty miles away.

Even though Scotland had no opposition, the referee blew the whistle to start the game . . . and then blew it again three seconds later to end it. The Scots were furious – another twenty minutes and they reckoned they might have scored. By the time Estonia did turn up two hours later – in readiness for the original evening kick-off – Scotland had long gone. Caught between a rock and a hard place, FIFA ordered the tie to be replayed at a neutral venue and the two teams met in Monaco four months later when, with Scotland's attack about as penetrating as a Sally Gunnell interview, the game ended in a tedious 0–0 draw. In truth, the Estonians need not have bothered turning up in Monaco either.

SHITE FACT

Following England's 1–0 victory over Argentina in Sapporo in 2002, Trevor Sinclair walked out of the stadium and boarded the opposition's team bus by mistake. 'There were not too many smiles around when I walked on,' he recalled, after admitting that he had temporarily lost his sense of direction in the midst of the England celebrations. 'Their guys were not too thrilled and I made a sharp exit.'

I PREDICT A RIOT

THE SOCCER WAR

The World Cup does everything bigger than other football competitions. So when it came to crowd trouble, it wasn't merely a case of a handful of Neanderthals wading into each other outside the local KFC – it was a full-blown war.

Back in 1969, Honduras and El Salvador were neighbours stricken by economic strife and mutual hatred. As fate would have it, they were also drawn to play each other over two legs in the qualifying tournament for the 1970 World Cup. The first leg took place in the Honduran capital of Tegucigalpa. The visiting Salvadoran team were treated to a cacophony of music, car horns and fireworks outside their hotel throughout the night before the game. It was what passed for Honduran hospitality. Given their opponents' lack of sleep, it came as little surprise that Honduras won 1–0 the next day in a match marred by rioting between rival fans. Worse still, a young Salvadoran, eighteen-year-old Amelia Bolanios, took her own life by shooting herself while watching the match on television. She was given a state funeral and became a martyr for the Salvadoran cause. The second leg was staged in San Salvador a week later. The Honduran players were horrified to discover that rotten eggs and dead rats had been thrown into their hotel rooms. Clearly it was only a three-star Salvadoran hotel. At the match itself, there was further rioting and the Honduran flag was symbolically set alight and replaced with a dirty rag. El Salvador won 3–0 and, with the aggregate score immaterial, the tie went to a third game. That was played in neutral Mexico City where El Salvador won through 3–2 in front of a massive police presence. With even the most diehard fan reluctant to take liberties with the Mexican police, the event passed off relatively peacefully, but it was merely the lull before the storm. Two weeks later, with tensions running high, the Salvadoran airforce tried to bomb Tegucigalpa airport – the 'Soccer War', as it became known, had kicked off. Ultimately it only lasted for a hundred hours, but the number of casualties (mostly civilians) still reached 3,000. Who said football was only a game?

SHITE FACT

The 1994 second-round tie between Mexico and Bulgaria was held up for fifteen minutes after the crossbar snapped. Officials had to fetch a replacement goal frame.

10 WORLD CUP DISTURBANCES

After Uruguay beat Argentina in the 1930 final, an aggrieved Argentinian mob stoned the Uruguayan embassy in Buenos Aires until police opened fire.

During the 1934 final between Czechoslovakia and host nation Italy, play was held up while police rescued one of the Czech players whose hair was being pulled by Italian fans through the wire fence at Rome's Stadio del Partito Nazionale Fascista.

When Brazilian star Garrincha was sent off during his country's 4–2 semi-final victory over host nation Chile in 1962, he was hit by a bottle thrown from the crowd as he left the pitch.

In the African qualifying zone for the 1974 World Cup, Nigeria's home game with Ghana was abandoned after eighty-seven minutes as a result of crowd trouble. Ghana were leading 3–2 at the time and were eventually awarded a 2–0 victory.

After Zimbabwe had lost a 1994 qualifier to Egypt in Cairo, they protested that their players had been struck by missiles thrown from the crowd. FIFA ordered the match to be replayed on neutral territory. The replay ended 0–0, allowing Zimbabwe to top the group.

In July 2000, during a World Cup qualifier, players from Zimbabwe and South Africa were forced to lie face down on the pitch when police in Harare fired tear gas into the crowd after bottles were hurled onto the pitch following South Africa's second goal. Thirteen people died in the resulting stampede, and the match was later abandoned.

Egypt tried unsuccessfully to have their 2001 qualifier against Algeria replayed after the 1–1 draw in Annaba was held up by stone-throwing fans.

Following Russia's 1–0 defeat to Japan in the 2002 finals, thousands of fans went on the rampage in Moscow, leaving two people dead and many injured.

North Korean soldiers and riot police had to intervene after violence erupted when the home side lost a World Cup qualifying match to Iran in March 2005. Bottles, stones and chairs were hurled on to the pitch in Pyongyang after a North Korean player was sent off for pushing the referee. The unrest continued after the final whistle and match officials were unable to leave the pitch for more than twenty minutes as objects were being thrown at them.

In September 2005, Zambian fans began rioting in Lusaka after their national team lost a qualifier to Senegal. Targetting an area containing a number of Senegalese residents, the trouble-makers destroyed a mosque and four houses, and also burned several cars.

HE SAID WHAT?

'He's literally got no right foot.'
David Pleat on US winger Preki, who favoured his left foot, at the 1998 World Cup

THANK YOU FOR THE MUSIC... NOT!

As sure as night follows day and Scotland go home after the first round, every World Cup has a song that is more irritating than a testicular rash. In the case of the British nations, the relentless optimism of the lyrics is matched only by the near certainty that they will never actually be fulfilled. And the quality of the singing gives a new meaning to the phrase 'flat back four'.

It all started for the England World Cup Squad in 1970 (Lonnie Donegan showing off his 'World Cup Willie' in 1966 doesn't count – besides he was Scottish) with that rousing anthem 'Back Home', although this, too, was penned by two Scotsmen – Bill Martin and Phil Coulter:

> *Back home, they'll be watching and waiting*
> *And cheering every move.*
> *Back home, though they think we're the greatest*
> *That's what we've got to prove.*

This was stirring stuff and stayed at number one for three weeks, but unfortunately the lyrics failed to take into account the fact that Gordon Banks would be suspiciously struck down with a stomach bug on the eve of the quarter-final or that his replacement, Peter Bonetti, would display all the agility of a beached whale. There was more chance of keeping a clean sheet in the incontinence ward at Mexico General Hospital. Ultimately, Bobby Moore and co. found it easier to top the charts than to topple the Germans.

England's failure to reach either the 1974 or 1978 finals at least spared the nation's eardrums from being subjected to further vocal torture (there was always Tina Charles for that), but Scotland nobly stepped into the breach in '78 with 'Ally's Tartan

The 1978 Scotland squad. Surprisingly, only one was a cardboard cut-out.

Army' by Andy Cameron. Boldly predicting how Scotland were going to win the World Cup, it somehow said everything about the misguided mission to Argentina, although even the English had to acknowledge:

> *We're representing Britain,*
> *And we're gaunny do or die.*
> *England cannae do it,*
> *'Cos they didnae qualify.*

Maybe not, but they would have beaten Iran.

Every World Cup squad has one player who thinks he can sing and in 1982 it was Kevin Keegan, fresh from his nauseating solo single 'Head Over Heels in Love'. In truth, Keegan was to singing what Pavarotti was to tricky wing play, but neverthless he led the vocals on 'This Time (We'll Get It Right)', backed by the likes of Paul Mariner, whose own dodgy hairdo gave him the look

of a lost member of Foreigner, Survivor or REO Speedwagon.
The song began:

> *We're on our way*
> *We are Ron's twenty-two*
> *Hear the roar,*
> *Of the red, white and blue.*

From such an unpromising opening it got steadily worse, but
still reached number two in the charts, kept off the top spot by,
among others, Spitting Image's 'The Chicken Song'. The
England team also missed out on glory, partly because Keegan
was injured . . . possibly by someone who had heard him sing.

Scotland also made it to Spain in 1982, prompting B. A.
Robertson and John Gordon Sinclair to record 'We Have a
Dream', though it turned out that 'Nightmare' would have better
described the team's actual performance in the tournament.

Undaunted, the England World Cup Squad tried again in
1986 with 'We've Got The Whole World At Our Feet'. Only its
highest chart position brought back memories of England's finest
hour – 66.

Reeling from the critical mauling of the 1986 effort and
perhaps sensing that the world was not yet ready for an album
entitled 'Graham Kelly Sings', the FA teamed the England
players with New Order for the 1990 official song 'World in
Motion'. It featured a solo from John Barnes in the days when he
thought he was a streetwise rapper:

> *Catch me if you can*
> *'Cause I'm the England man*
> *And what you're looking for*
> *Is the master plan.*

Like most rappers on the street, it should have been consigned
to the nearest bin.

Meanwhile, the Republic of Ireland's official song for 1990

was 'Put 'Em Under Pressure', a production that boasts the unique credits of music by U2, vocals by Jack Charlton.

The 1998 World Cup resulted in embarrassment all round. Despite, or perhaps because of, enlisting the help of the Spice Girls to sing on England United's 'On Top of the World', the official song was overshadowed by Fat Les's 'Vindaloo' and the reworked version of 'Three Lions'. North of the border, Del Amitri wooed the Scottish players with 'Don't Come Home Too Soon'. As usual, they did.

For 2002, Ant and Dec were chosen to perform 'We're On The Ball', which contained such excruciating lines as:

> *Send an SOS, a country's in need.*
> *Sven's the man, he's got a plan*
> *We've found that super Swede.*

Perhaps it was meant to be ironic.

At the time of writing, England's official 2006 World Cup song remains under wraps. Given Sven's likely formation, perhaps a cover version of 'Flying Without Wings' would make appropriate listening . . . with the sound turned down of course.

SHITE FACT

When female supporters went to watch the Republic of Ireland play Iran in the second leg of their 2001 World Cup play-off at the Azadi Stadium, Tehran, it was the first time that women had been allowed into the stadium since Iran's 1979 Islamic Revolution.

HALL OF SHAME

SATURDAY NIGHT HAY FEVER

For years now drugs and sport have been increasingly linked, particularly in the Tour de France, which has brought a whole new meaning to the term 'peddling drugs'. Whereas Popeye used to make do with spinach, performance-enhancing drugs have become alarmingly common in many fields of sport with the notable exception of Britain's women tennis players, who have clearly not taken anything to improve their performance over the past thirty years. Football has managed to stay – on the surface at least – relatively clean, although you may wonder what Graham Taylor was on when he kept picking Carlton Palmer for England during the early 1990s. But back at the 1978 World Cup, Scotland were hit by a drug-taking scandal that almost threatened to overshadow their ineptitude on the pitch.

The summer of 1978 saw John Travolta as the world's number-one entertainer and, even more bizarrely, Scotland as Britain's number-one football team, for the Scots had succeeded in qualifying for the World Cup finals in Argentina where the other three home nations had failed. That Wales missed out was scarcely a surprise – there's usually as much chance of them reaching the finals as Anne Robinson being given the Freedom of Swansea. The same went for Northern Ireland, but England's absence prompted scenes of rejoicing not seen again north of the border until Gordon Brown found a five-pence piece on the terraces at Raith Rovers.

Thus the Tartan Army arrived in Argentina in high spirits – mostly from the Duty Free shop – and encouraged by manager Ally MacLeod's assertion that Scotland could actually win the World Cup. Alas, Ally was no Mystic Meg, and in their opening game Scotland were humbled 3–1 by a Peru team that had supposedly seen better days. Compared to what went on in Cordoba, Culloden was one of Scotland's better days.

Worse was to follow. Whereas the rest of Scotland had been gripped by World Cup fever, winger Willie Johnston had apparently been gripped by hay fever. It was Johnston's misfortune to be picked for a random dope test after the Peru game, along with teammate Kenny Dalglish and the Scots' Peruvian tormentor, two-goal Teófilo Cubillas. 'We all pissed in the bottle,' remembered Johnston ruefully, 'and theirs was a lot clearer than mine.' The test proved positive. Johnston claimed that he had taken two Fencamfamin pills to combat his hay fever and help him sleep better. But his explanation was as cloudy as his sample and, already boasting a disciplinary record that meant he'd been on his knees before the FA more often than Faria Alam, he was sent home in disgrace and banned from international football for a year. Scotland's World Cup dream was over before it had begun.

HE SAID WHAT?

'It's not chasing women and having sex that tires out young footballers. It's staying up all night looking for it.'

Nigeria coach Clemens Westerhof at the 1994 World Cup

YOU'VE BEEN FRAMED

When Sir Alf Ramsey opted to take England on an acclimatizing tour of South America prior to the 1970 World Cup finals in Mexico, you knew it was a decision that he had not taken lightly. For Ramsey only had to pass a travel agent's to break out in a rash. He despised all things foreign – he could hardly bear to set foot in Scotland – and was not renowned for his desire to

Alf Ramsey trusted foreigners like a spring lamb trusts a master butcher.

embrace other cultures. To Ramsey, *Viva España* was a Madrid Vauxhall dealership. The unseemly spat with Argentina four years earlier was still fresh in his mind, so under normal circumstances warm-up games in Colombia and Ecuador would have been well down his list of 'things to do', probably just below having a leg amputated. But this was the World Cup and, as defending champions, England had to be prepared for the altitude problems they would encounter in Mexico.

On arrival in the Colombian capital, Bogotá, Ramsey issued a few useful local tips for his players that could have come straight from the city's tourist brochure . . .

- Don't drink the water.
- Don't eat the food.
- Don't go near street traders.
- Visit only reputable shops.
- Don't go anywhere alone – not even the toilet.
- Don't go out after dark.
- Don't talk to strangers.

With the players thus relaxed, a few browsed around a jewellery shop called Fuego Verde (Green Fire), which was situated in the foyer of the team's Tequendama Hotel. Having seen nothing worth buying, Bobby Moore and Bobby Charlton had just wandered back into the hotel foyer when they were suddenly asked to return to the shop. Inside, they were informed that an emerald and diamond bracelet was missing. Realizing that they were being accused, the pair volunteered to be searched but the offer was declined and the police were summoned instead. Alerted to the situation, Ramsey immediately smelled a veritable plague of rats.

After formal statements had been made to the police, the two Bobbies were free to play against Colombia and Ecuador later in the week. That seemed to be the end of the matter until, on the party's return to Bogotá to change planes en route to Mexico, Moore was arrested. When news of the England captain's predicament reached these shores, there was widespread disbelief. After all, what possible interest could Bobby Moore have in a piece of gaudy jewellery . . . apart from the fact that he was an Essex boy? But what seemed truly preposterous was the fact that the Colombians were accusing Bobby Charlton of being Moore's accomplice. It is hard to imagine a less likely thief. Bobby Charlton had a reputation that made Mother Teresa look shady.

After three days of being held under house arrest, Moore was brought to face his accuser, twenty-one-year-old shop assistant Clara Padilla, for a reconstruction of the alleged crime. The shop owner, Danilo Rojas, was also in attendance, as was a Colombian rent-a-witness who claimed to have seen the footballer steal the bracelet. At the reconstruction, Padilla confidently stated that she had seen Moore put the bracelet in the left pocket of his England leisure suit. She was absolutely sure. No mistake. Final answer. At this, Moore, who was wearing the same suit, calmly revealed that there was no pocket on the left. Perhaps she should have gone 50:50.

Their case in tatters, one might have expected the Colombians to admit defeat graciously, but the charges against Moore were not dropped for another five years, and even then it was only for lack of evidence. This in itself was unexpected, to learn that Colombian justice relied on evidence.

The popular theory is that Moore had been framed in an attempt to put him out of the World Cup or at the very least to unsettle him. To his credit, he was at his most composed throughout the tournament, playing as if the threat hanging over him was nothing more than a parking fine. But the episode did nothing to cure Alf Ramsey's mistrust of Johnny Foreigner and in particular of South Americans. Corned beef remained firmly off limits in the Ramsey household.

SHITE FACT

Cameroon's Samuel Eto'o took two and a half hours to pass water for a routine dope test after the 2002 World Cup tie against Saudi Arabia. While officials waited anxiously, reporters tried to encourage him by making waterfall sounds.

DOSSIER DON DEFECTS

There was a nasty side to British football in the 1970s and the nastiest side of all was Leeds United. Without doubt they possessed some hugely talented players, but their overall legacy

Don Revie was about as welcome as a French kiss at a funeral.

was one of intimidation, borderline cheating and brutality. Journalists preferred to call them 'cynical' . . . in the same way that Vlad the Impaler was cynical. The man behind the Yorkshire side's success and unpopularity was manager Don Revie, viewed in many quarters as the evil genius who was trying to destroy the beautiful game. Although Revie seemed to wear the permanent expression of someone whose dog had just been run over, nobody could dispute his managerial record. So he was the obvious choice to succeed Sir Alf Ramsey as permanent England boss, the FA hoping that he could achieve at national level what he had done at club level . . . but preferably without the GBH.

However, Revie's methods did not exactly endear him to all of the England players. A stickler for detail, he was renowned for preparing lengthy dossiers on the opposition, thus earning the nickname 'Dossier Don'. These told everything you needed to know about the modern professional footballer – his favourite hair-styling mousse, which supermarkets he had recently opened, and so on. At Leeds, Revie's players hung on his every word, but there weren't too many Leeds players in the England squad since even Revie's ability to bend the rules didn't extend to acquiring English citizenship for Billy Bremner, Johnny Giles and Eddie Gray. So when Revie's England failed to qualify for the 1976 European Championships, he found no shortage of critics – from both inside and outside his squad.

The qualifying groups for the 1978 World Cup teamed England with Italy, Finland and Luxembourg, with only one country advancing to the next stage. Finland were despatched home and away (albeit in unconvincing fashion at Wembley) and Luxembourg were predictably swept aside, but the crunch game in Rome in November 1976 saw England on the wrong end of a 2–0 scoreline. Nevertheless with two games to play – including the crucial return fixture against Italy – there was still an outside chance that England could qualify. But Revie didn't bother waiting around to find out. In July 1977 he sensationally resigned as England manager and attempted to secure a pay-off from the FA while conveniently forgetting to tell his bosses that he had already lined up a lucrative contract to coach the United Arab Emirates. The public branded him a traitor and a mercenary, and the FA suspended him on a charge of bringing the game into disrepute, an accusation that he subsequently overturned in court. But he never managed in England again, instead becoming the country's most infamous exile, along with Ronnie Biggs. Indeed there was probably more chance of Biggs landing a job as a security guard in England than there was of Revie finding coaching work here. In the wake of his resignation, there were calls for the FA to choose Brian Clough as Revie's successor, but, with an ego the size of a small country, Clough was better suited to handling/bullying lesser players than international stars. Having said that, the ride would have been interesting. Clough may not have filled the FA's trophy cabinet, but he would probably have emptied their drinks cabinet.

SHITE FACT

At the age of seventeen, Cameroon's Rigobert Song became the youngest player to be sent off in a World Cup finals match when he was dismissed against Brazil in June 1994. His debut was greeted with the immortal line: 'They're playing R. Song.' The Cameroonian also holds the record for being the only player to be sent off in successive finals tournaments; he was red-carded against Chile in France '98.

MARADONA BUSTED

There are some scary sights in football. You wouldn't want to meet Iain Dowie down a dark alley, or worse still in broad daylight. And Wayne Rooney has the sort of face that only a

Diego Maradona found that things go better with coke.

grandmother could love. But nothing can compare with the wild-eyed, teeth-baring monster that snarled into the lens of a TV camera during the 1994 World Cup finals. It was, of course, none other than that diminutive dynamo Diego Maradona, who had taken so many drugs he was now higher than Peter Crouch.

SHITE FACT

The record defeat in a World Cup finals match was the 10–1 loss suffered by El Salvador at the hands of Hungary in 1982. In the course of the rout László Kiss became the first substitute to score a hat-trick in the finals. Never has a kiss been so unwelcome in El Salvador.

A hero in Argentina following the 1986 World Cup and the notorious 'Hand of God' incident, Maradona's public decline began in 1991 when he tested positive for cocaine and was charged with supplying drugs, as a result of which he was banned from all competitions for fifteen months. Given the abuse meted out to his body, it was feared that he would be a fish out of water at the 1994 finals. The once slippery eel had been replaced by a bloater. Indeed he looked decidedly lethargic in the play-offs against Australia, only to have made seemingly miraculous strides by the time the finals came around. Shortly after taking pot shots at a group of journalists with an air rifle – the sort of action that could earn a jail sentence in some countries and a knighthood in others – the thirty-four-year-old took to the field for Argentina's opening match with Greece. The Argentines cruised to a 4–0 victory and his performance suggested that, if not quite back to his best, he was at least more than the tired old Maradona tribute band that most people had been expecting. More impressive still, he showed remarkable stamina in Argentina's second game, lasting the full ninety minutes against Nigeria. But just as the world prepared to hail his comeback, he was required to take a standard dope test, which revealed five different variants of the stimulant ephedrine . . . Using an old line (perhaps his regular dealer wasn't in town), he claimed the banned substances formed part of a cold medication. The Argentine FA didn't buy it and immediately withdrew him from the tournament.

Maradona later declared himself a full-blown drug addict and admitted to having used cocaine since 1982. He became involved with prostitutes and shadowy gangland figures and his weight ballooned to nineteen stone. In Argentina there was a sense of mourning; in England there was a sense of quiet satisfaction. The Hand of God moves in mysterious ways.

SHITE FACT

Luis Monti appeared in two consecutive World Cup finals . . . but for two different countries. In 1930 he was a member of the beaten Argentine team, but he enjoyed better fortune four years later when he switched his allegiance to Italy.

YOUR SHITE GERMAN WORLD CUP DICTIONARY

Alarmed by jolly German fans chanting 'We're going to invade you again' during a 2005 match with Slovakia, and by fears that they would bait the English fans with cries of '*Inselaffen*' (Island Monkeys), the German authorities have launched a charm offensive ahead of the 2006 World Cup. The campaign is intended to banish the stereotypes of mullets and thigh-slapping Bavarians, and points out that goose-stepping is actually illegal in modern Germany. In addition, London's Goethe Institute launched a language course for English fans travelling to the World Cup or 'Weltmeisterschaft'. For those unable to attend the course, here are our own helpful words and phrases with their German translations:

Useful nouns
added-on time – *Nachspielzeit*
attacking play – *Angriffsspiel*
back-heel – *Hackentrick*
ball – *Ball*
ball control – *Ballführung*
banana shot – *Bananenflanke*
bicycle kick – *Fallrückzieher*
bogey team – *Angstgegner*
captain – *Mannschaftsführer*
corner – *Eckball, Ecke*
cross – *Flanke*
defender – *Abwehrspieler*
dive – *Hechtsprung*
diving header – *Flugkopfball*
draw – *Auslosung*
equalizer – *Ausgleich*
extra time – *Verlängerung*

fan – *Anhänger*
final score – *Endstand*
flat back four – *flachen Viererkette*
foul – *Foul, Foulspiel*
free kick – *Freistoß*
goal – *Tor, Treffer*
goalkeeper – *Torwart*
goal kick – *Abschlag*
goalscorer – *Torschütze*
half-time – *Halbzeit(pause)*
halfway line – *Mittellinie*
header – *Kopfball*
hooligan – *Krawallmacher*
individual effort – *Einzelaktion*
kick-off – *Anpfiff*
linesman – *Linienrichter*
linesman's flag – *Fahne*
man-for-man marking – *Manndeckung*
middle-finger salute – *Stinkefinger*
midfield – *Mittelfeld*
nutmeg – *Beinschuss*
offside – *Abseits*
offside goal – *Abseitstreffer*
offside position – *Abseitsstellung*
offside trap – *Abseitsfalle*
one-two – *Doppelpass*
own goal – *Eigentor*
penalty – *Elfmeter, Strafstoß*
penalty area – *Strafraum*
penalty shoot-out – *Elfmeterschießen*
red card – *rote Karte*
referee – *Schiedsrichter*
save – *Parade*
shot – *Schuss*
shot against the post – *Pfostenschuss*
side-netting – *Außennetz*
sliding tackle – *Grätsche*
striker – *Stürmer*
substitute – *Auswechselspieler*

sweeper – *Ausputzer*
tackle – *Tackling*
teammate – *Mitspieler*
through ball – *Steilpass*
throw-in – *Einwurf*
unmarked – *ungedeckt*
wall (defensive) – *Mauer*
winger – *Außenstürmer*
winning goal – *Siegtor*
yellow card – *gelbe Karte*

Valuable verbs
to attack – *angreifen*
to blow the final whistle – *abpfeifen*
to commit a professional foul – *notbremse ziehen*
to dribble – *dribbeln*
to head in – *einköpfen*
to tackle – *angehen*

Functional phrases
A game of two halves – *ein Spiel von zwei Hälften*
At the end of the day – *letzten Endes*
Off! Off! Off! – *Platzverweis!*
Our team was robbed – *das ist nicht fair, wir hätten gewinnen müssen*
Over the moon – *überglücklich*
Ref, we know where your car is – *Schiri, wir wissen wo dein Auto steht*
Same old Germans, always cheating – *die Deutschen mogeln wie
    üblich*
Sick as a parrot – *kotzübel sein*
Who are you? – *wer bist du?*
Who's the bastard in the black? – *wer ist der Scheißkerl, den
    Schwarz gekleidet ist?*
You only sing when you're winning – *ihr singt nur, wenn ihr gewinnt*
You're crap and you know you are – *ihr seht ja ein, ihr seid Scheiße*
You're not singing any more – *ihr singt nicht mehr*

TIFFS AND TANTRUMS ⚽

THE INCREDIBLE SULK

Secretly a lot of English men envy Italians – their food, their wine, their country, their reputation as great lovers. Everything about Italians oozes style and class. They have Chianti, we have Carling Black Label; they have lasagne, we have mushy peas; they have Gucci, we have Milletts; they had Sophia Loren, we had Glenda Jackson. The Italians even went one better when it came to taking penalties, for whereas England went out of two successive World Cups (1990 and 1998, having failed to qualify in 1994) on penalties, the Italians crashed out in three successive penalty shoot-outs – 1990, 1994 and 1998. Unless you were wearing lederhosen in 1966, it was the most unwanted hat-trick in the history of the World Cup.

At the 2002 finals, Italy negotiated their group with customary discomfort, just managing to edge out Croatia and Ecuador, but finishing three points adrift of Mexico. This set them up for a second-round clash with hosts South Korea who had already surpassed expectations by topping their group. After Ahn Jung-Hwan had missed a fourth-minute penalty, Italy went ahead on eighteen minutes through Christian Vieri, but nobody in the Italian camp relaxed, for David Blunkett is better at holding on to a lead than the Italians. They spurned further chances until, with just two minutes remaining, Seol Ki-Hyeon equalized for South Korea. Still the Italians had a chance to win it in normal time, only for Vieri to miss from five yards in the dying seconds. And so the tie went to 'Golden Goal', where Italy's frustration at their own shortcomings and those of the match officials began to boil over. First, Vieri had a seemingly good goal disallowed for offside. Then Francesco Totti was sent off after receiving a second yellow card for diving, even though he looked to have been fouled. To rub salt into the wounds, Ahn grabbed a sensational winner for South Korea just four minutes before the Italians would have been subjected to yet another penalty shoot-out. Some of their fans may almost have been relieved.

The Italians felt hard done by. They smashed up their dressing room and complained about corruption, a subject on which they are the world's acknowledged experts. Back in Rome, irate fans chanted 'death to the referee' (Ecuador's Byron Moreno who was subsequently axed by FIFA), and shouted 'Thieves, thieves, you stole the game' at a small group of South Korean supporters. By a cruel twist of fate, Korea's match-winner Ahn plied his trade with Italian club Perugia – a fact that was not lost on Perugia president Luciano Gaucci who accused Ahn of biting the hand that feeds him. Gaucci raged: 'He will never set foot in Perugia again. He was a phenomenon only when he played against Italy. I am a nationalist and I regard such behaviour not only as an affront to Italian pride, but also an offence to a country

South Korea's Ahn Jung-Hwan (right) hurt Italian pride at the 2002 World Cup.

which two years ago opened its doors to him. I have no intention of paying a salary to someone who has ruined Italian soccer.' When it was pointed out to Gaucci that his draconian measure was immoral and in all probability illegal, he backed down and the ban on Ahn was lifted. Gaucci's toys were quietly put back in his pram.

HE SAID WHAT?

'The referee was a disgrace, absolutely scandalous. I've never seen a game like it. It seemed as if they just sat around a table and decided to throw us out.'

Franco Frattini, Italy's minister for public offences, moaning about referee Byron Moreno after the controversial defeat to South Korea in 2002

ABSENT FRIENDS

With the possible exception of the Dingles of *Emmerdale* and the Windsors of The Mall, the FIFA nations must be the world's most dysfunctional family. Right from the inaugural World Cup back in 1930, the tournament has been beset by playground bickering along the lines of 'our stadium's bigger than your stadium' and 'I'll get our Head of Footballing Development on to you'. Six countries applied to host the first competition – Italy, Holland, Hungary, Spain, Sweden and Uruguay. The last-named were eventually chosen, partly because 1930 was the centenary of their independence, but also because, as Olympic soccer champions in 1924 and 1928, they were the uncrowned champions of the world. Furthermore, they promised to build a brand new stadium in which to stage the final and to pay the hotel and travelling expenses of all participating nations. Those were four good reasons for picking Uruguay, whereas all Holland could offer by way of inducement was 'no hills to climb'. But the snubbed five took rejection badly and refused to journey to South America, a trip that was, in fairness, a ridiculously long three weeks. Of course modern technology means that nowadays it can take just three weeks to travel from London to somewhere just outside Manchester by Virgin Trains. When Austria, Czechoslovakia, Germany and Switzerland also withdrew, the opening World Cup was left with only thirteen participants (unlucky for some), including a mere four from Europe – France, Belgium, Romania and Yugoslavia. No British team took part as they had all pulled out of FIFA in 1928 following a row over payments to amateurs.

It is never wise to decline South American hospitality and the snubbed Uruguayans harboured the grudge for the next twenty years, which by their standards made it just a minor tiff. They refused to travel to Italy for the 1934 World Cup, while Argentina – angry that the Italians had poached three of their best players – sent a weakened squad. To add to the chaos Chile qualified but withdrew, Romania were disqualified then reinstated, and Mexico travelled all the way to Rome, only to be eliminated in a play-off against the USA three days before the finals began.

Uruguay were still sulking when the World Cup went to France in 1938 and were joined in their umbrage by Argentina, who were insulted that their own candidature had been over-looked in favour of the French. Argentina's decision to stay at home prompted a riot outside their federation's offices in Buenos Aires. By now soccer fans were really beginning to get the hang of this rioting lark. At least Austria had a valid reason for with-drawing at the last minute after their country and their best players had been annexed by Germany.

Uruguay finally returned to the fold in 1950, when the tourna-ment was held on their doorstep in Brazil, but Argentina again refused to play ball, having fallen out with the Brazilian Federation. After losing a qualifying tie 7–0 to Turkey, Syria declined to play the return game, whereupon Turkey decided they couldn't be bothered to travel to Brazil. France had already been eliminated in another group but were offered a place on Turkey's withdrawal. However, when the French saw their arduous travel itinerary, which meant flights of 2,000 miles between matches, they threatened to pull out unless it was amended. The Brazilian Federation stood firm and France stayed at home. Naturally, while every other competing nation was expected to travel the length and breadth of the country, the organizers had ensured that Brazil had the luxury of playing all but one of their six matches in Rio.

The four British associations had returned to the FIFA fold in 1946 and were now given their very own qualifying group with two countries progressing to the finals. Despite this, the Scottish FA loftily announced that they would only be sending a team to Brazil if Scotland qualified as outright British champions. Ultimately, though, the Scots finished runners-up to England and refused to compromise. Portugal were then offered Scotland's place, but it turned out that they were washing their hair that night. It had proved easier to find guests for Hitler's Farewell Bunker Party than to persuade teams to go to the 1950 World Cup, and once again the competition went ahead with just thirteen teams taking part.

One country that did want to compete were India . . . but only on condition that they could play barefoot. They had played well without boots at the 1948 Olympics and had received a bye to the World Cup finals after all their opponents obligingly withdrew. But FIFA's insistence that footwear was a necessity forced India to step down, effectively booting them out . . .

Although all sixteen African countries withdrew from the 1966 qualifying tournament, the shenanigans of old have become less common over the past thirty years. Mexico were kicked out of the 1990 World Cup as punishment for fielding three overage players in an international under-20 tournament, and in 1974 the USSR were disqualified despite winning their qualifying group. They were drawn to meet Chile in a play-off and after the first leg in Moscow ended 0–0, the Soviets refused to play the return in Santiago's National Stadium on the grounds that it had housed prisoners during a recent military coup orchestrated by the notorious General Pinochet. FIFA rejected the USSR's request to play the match at a neutral venue, leaving Chile to line up against no opposition before 40,000 fans and walk the ball into an empty net. The match was then abandoned. If only Scotland had managed to pull that off in Estonia twenty-two years later.

SHITE FACT

Whereas other members of the Belgian squad at the 2002 World Cup had to share hotel rooms, defender Daniel Van Buyten was given a room of his own . . . apparently due to his 'disturbing sleep talk'.

GREAVSIE DOES A RUNNER

Jimmy Greaves and Alf Ramsey were about as comfortable in each other's presence as Titus Bramble and Jean-Alain Boumsong. Ramsey liked players that he could fit into a system, who would obey orders without question and would run tirelessly for the cause. A team of eleven robots would have suited him nicely, particularly if one of them had its metal teeth missing. It followed, therefore, that he had no time for flair players who might, on a good day, turn a game with a moment's brilliance. Ramsey viewed such mavericks with suspicion, reasoning that they could not always be relied upon to produce the goods. Rather like an ashtray on a motorbike, they were a luxury. In Ramsey's eyes, Greaves fell into that category.

Greaves was without doubt the most natural English goalscorer of his generation. To compare Liverpool's Roger Hunt with him would be to put Cilla Black on a par with Maria Callas. Yet Ramsey never really appreciated Greaves either as a player or as a person, possibly because Greaves possessed a wicked wit, whereas Ramsey's own sense of humour was one of the best-kept secrets of the twentieth century.

England lift the World Cup – but without Jimmy Greaves,
who was reduced to watching from the stand.

Greaves and Hunt were paired up front for England's opening game at the 1966 World Cup, but neither got any change out of a resolute Uruguayan defence and the match ended in a disappointing goalless draw, the one saving grace of which was that television replays had yet to become widespread. Hunt was on target in the second game – a 2–0 victory over Mexico – but again Greaves failed to sparkle. Hunt, still more carthorse than thoroughbred, then scored both goals in the 2–0 defeat of France, a match in which Greaves picked up an injury. This was a stroke of good fortune for Ramsey who, while never afraid to make unpopular decisions, knew the risk of a public backlash if he dropped Greaves. Fortunately for Ramsey, however, Greaves's injury took the pressure off him, and he was able to call up Geoff Hurst for the quarter-final with Argentina.

By the time England had reached the final, Greaves was fit again and raring to play, but Hurst, who had scored the winner against Argentina, and been instrumental in the semi-final victory over Portugal, was already too important to the team to make way for the returning Greaves. The only possible candidate to make way for Greaves was Hunt, but Ramsey, despite having taken elocution lessons in the past to correct his Dagenham accent, was still more likely to drop his aitches than to drop Hunt. Greaves took the news of his omission badly. The World Cup final should have been the greatest day of his life, but instead it turned out to be one of the worst. Rather than remain with the squad, he packed his bags and went home shortly after the game. He was even too distraught to attend the post-match celebration. There can only be one reason for that: he hadn't heard the drinks were free.

HE SAID WHAT?

'We needed Winston Churchill, and we got Iain Duncan Smith.'

*An England defender bemoaning Sven's lack of passion
at half-time during the 2002 quarter-final against Brazil*

SHITE FACT

After losing 2–1 to Puerto Rico in a 1992 qualifier, the Dominican Republic tried to claim that the entire Puerto Rican squad were ineligible because they had US passports.

BAD BOYS

Burkino Faso's players refused to play a World Cup qualifier with Zimbabwe in July 2001 following a row over bonuses. The players said they wouldn't board the plane to Harare because they still hadn't received promised bonuses from an earlier match with South Africa. Instead, Burkino Faso's under-17 team were sent to Zimbabwe and performed admirably before losing 1–0.

Prior to the 1962 finals, Spain's Real Madrid star Alfredo di Stefano was involved in an ongoing feud with national coach Helenio Herrera. Di Stefano withdrew from the squad before the start of the tournament, claiming that he had pulled a muscle. Perhaps he did it while stamping his feet in a tantrum.

When winger Renato Gaúcho sneaked back to Brazil's training camp after curfew, coach Tele Santana threw him out of the squad for the 1986 finals. The decision so upset his friend and Flamengo teammate Leandro that he didn't turn up to catch the team plane from Rio to Mexico.

Northern Ireland's Phil Mulryne and Jeff Whitley were sent home after breaching curfew rules and indulging in a marathon drinking session in Belfast four days before the September 2005 qualifying tie with Azerbaijan.

German midfielder Stefan Effenberg was sent packing from the 1994 finals for giving the finger to disgruntled German fans as he was being substituted during the unconvincing 3–2 victory over South Korea.

Kenya coach Mohammed Kheri threatened to boycott his team's 2005 qualifying match against Malawi in a row over pay. He claimed he was owed around £15,000 in salary and allowances. Eventually he backed down.

Several members of the Ethiopia squad that was bound for a 1992 qualifier in Casablanca mysteriously vanished when their plane stopped over in Rome. All but eleven of the Ethiopian contigent disappeared, which left the football side with just nine recognized players, and so to make up the numbers two team coaches had no choice but to take to the field against Morocco. The resulting match was abandoned after fifty-five minutes because Ethiopia, who were trailing 5–0, had five injured players and no substitutes and were therefore unable to field a complete team.

Uruguay goalkeeper Antonio Mazzali was axed from the 1930 World Cup squad for sneaking out of the team hotel. After being locked in isolation in a Montevideo hotel for nearly eight weeks, Mazzali could take no more and crept out one night to visit his family. Apprehended on his return, he was told that he could rejoin his family for good and would take no further part in the inaugural World Cup.

SHITE FACT

After beating France 1–0 at the 1930 finals, Argentina's players expected some form of acclaim. Instead the Uruguayan crowd chaired two French players shoulder-high off the pitch at the end of the game. The Argentines were so angry that they threatened to go home.

WHEN IRISH EYES WEREN'T SMILING

It would have required the combined forces of the Magnificent Seven, the Famous Five and the Special One to persuade Mick

McCarthy and Roy Keane to tolerate each other. There was less chance of them exchanging a civilized word than of Gary Neville receiving a Valentine's card with a Liverpool postmark. Apparently the feud dates back to 1992 when Keane, then the new boy in the Republic of Ireland squad, kept the team bus waiting before a friendly in Boston, Massachusetts. As one of the senior pros, McCarthy saw fit to blast Keane for being disrespectful to manager Jack Charlton. Keane gave it back in spades and while McCarthy probably thought little more about the incident, Keane never forgot a grudge – as Alf Inge Haaland later found to his cost.

SHITE FACT

Glasgow Rangers refused to release their players for Scotland's 1954 World Cup finals campaign because of a close-season club tour.

Keane's problems stemmed partly from the fact that he was playing for the wrong country. For most of his international career, with the possible exception of Paul McGrath, Keane was the only world-class player in the Republic team. He could have walked into virtually any other side, but it was his misfortune to have been one of the few to possess a genuine Irish passport and not have to rely on qualifying by dint of an English grandmother who had once drunk a bottle of Guinness. Under Jack Charlton the process became so farcical that tickets for *Riverdance* were often enough to secure Irish eligibility. Keane had little time for Charlton's approach, which invariably required the Irish to muddle through against the odds in a manner that made them so endearing, and he soon found that things were no better when McCarthy succeeded Charlton as manager. McCarthy and Charlton were hewn from the same rock – no-nonsense centre halves who kicked anything in their path as long as it wasn't the

HE SAID WHAT?

'I didn't rate you as a player, I don't rate you as a manager, and I don't rate you as a person. You're a f**king wanker and you can stick your World Cup up your arse.'

Roy Keane putting the boot into Irish boss Mick McCarthy

ball – and both men were about as Irish as Stalin. But, like Charlton before him, McCarthy enjoyed considerable success as Irish manager, leading them through a difficult group to qualify for the 2002 finals. They seemed one big happy family, but when McCarthy referred to Keane as his 'midfield anchor', you couldn't help wondering whether he was using rhyming slang.

The tensions between the two men resurfaced on the Pacific island of Saipan where the Irish were to spend a week preparing for the tournament. Keane, who had been accustomed to only the best at Manchester United, was horrified to find a bumpy pitch, no balls and no spare goalposts. And the special drinks that the Football Association of Ireland were supposedly providing to combat dehydration had yet to arrive. To Keane, it seemed that the show was being run by the Chuckle Brothers. And after a farce of a training match, with outfield players in goal, Keane stormed off to the team bus with a face longer than Ruud van Nistelrooy's. He said he'd had enough and was going home.

The fiery Irishman was persuaded to change his mind, but two days later he erupted again. McCarthy had read an inflammatory interview with Keane in the *Irish Times* and challenged the player to explain himself in front of the rest of the squad. Keane's chosen method of explanation was to call McCarthy a veritable thesaurus of derogatory adjectives, including 'spineless', 'gutless', 'incompetent' and 'ignorant'. But that was just for starters. When McCarthy hinted that Keane might have deliberately pulled out of a play-off game in Iran, the reply was a volley of four-letter words usually reserved for Gordon Ramsay casting his eyes over an unsatisfactory soufflé.

McCarthy promptly ordered him home although, rather like a guy who ditches his girlfriend after he has been caught sleeping with her best mate, it was a moot point as to who dumped whom. McCarthy went on to brand Keane a 'disruptive influence' . . . in much the same way that an Exocet missile landing in your back garden can be a disruptive influence. As for Keane, he said McCarthy 'can rot in hell'.

The rest of the Irish team united behind McCarthy and performed creditably in the World Cup, reaching the second round before going out to Spain on penalties. But when (still without Keane who was injured anyway) they made a poor start to qualifying for the 2004 European Championships, McCarthy resigned. Keane announced his retirement from international football shortly afterwards. It is not known whether the two men will ever talk to each other again but if so, given their past history, it is likely to be on an episode of *Trisha*.

SHITE FACT

In July 1993, Brazil lost a World Cup qualifying tie for the first time in their history, going down 2–0 to Bolivia. On their return home, the disgraced Brazilian squad were subjected to a torrent of abuse, and assistant coach Mario Zagallo had to be restrained by officials after a taxi driver had hurled insults at coach Carlos Alberto Parreira.

BARKING MAD

NO WAY, JOSÉ

If you wanted someone you could trust with your life, whom you could rely on in any situation, a Latin-American goalkeeper would feature slightly below the CEO of Enron and Jack the Ripper. Although to describe them as 'mad as a hatter' might offend Luton supporters, the truth is that, almost without exception, these guys are a breed apart.

Take José Luis Chilavert, the Paraguayan goalkeeper who possesses a goalscoring record that Jon Stead can only dream of. Like many Latin-American keepers, Chilavert has always been prone to going AWOL from his own penalty area, haring upfield to take free kicks and penalties. In 1996 alone, he scored eight goals for his club, Vélez Sársfield of Argentina, plus one for his country. In a league game against River Plate, he netted a spectacular 60-yard free kick, taken quickly after he spotted his opposing number, German Burgos, off his line. The two men met once more for an Argentina v. Paraguay World Cup qualifier in Buenos Aires in September 1996. In the build-up to the game, Chilavert, who was to diplomacy what Vanessa Feltz is to anorexia, rubbished Burgos and boasted that he would score again. So when Paraguay were awarded a free kick around 25 yards out, nobody was going to prevent Chilavert taking another potshot. Photographers behind the goal reckoned that Burgos was trembling as Chilavert lined up his strike, and although Burgos managed to get both hands on the ball, he allowed it to slip from his grasp and creep over the line. Chilavert's joy was unconfined.

Milking his fame, Chilavert took to wearing a goalkeeper's jersey bearing the image of a snarling bulldog. T-shirts featuring the bulldog sold in their thousands and the Paraguayan FA even

Paraguay keeper José Luis Chilavert never let his official goalkeeping duties affect his maverick goalscoring abilities.

staged a competition among Asunción pet owners to find the dog that looked most like the one on Chilavert's shirt. Meanwhile, the United States FA were apparently thinking of running a similar contest to find anyone with a goat that looked like Alexi Lalas.

Already voted World Goalkeeper of the Year in 1995 and 1997, Chilavert's cult status scaled new heights in 1999 when, playing for Vélez against Ferro Carril Oeste, he became the first goalkeeper in the history of football to score a hat-trick. He went on to spearhead Paraguay's qualification for the 2002 World Cup by scoring four goals, including two stunning free kicks in the 5–1 victory over Bolivia. On the downside he had a penalty saved against Chile and received a three-match ban for spitting on Brazil's Roberto Carlos. When he finally announced his retirement in 2004, he had scored a staggering sixty-two goals in his professional career, including eight at international level.

They say goalkeepers should always be committed and one who should definitely have been committed was Peru's Ramón Quiroga, the man at the centre of the Argentina v. Peru match-fixing allegation at the 1978 World Cup, and someone who loved to charge upfield for last-minute corners long before it became fashionable for goalkeepers to do so. In that respect he was at least fifteen years ahead of his time. Nicknamed 'El Loco' ('the Crazy One') by his long-suffering teammates, Quiroga made his mark in that tournament with a series of eccentric displays, none more so than in the second-round match against Poland. With Peru trailing 1–0 and just two minutes remaining, Quiroga suddenly appeared on the halfway line to tackle a Polish player and launch another attack. Seconds later, he halted another Polish breakaway by popping up well inside the Polish half, although on that occasion his rugby tackle on Grzegorz Lato earned him a booking. He thus went down in history as the first goalkeeper to be booked for a foul in his opponents' half, which was something to slip into conversation at dinner parties. Quiroga really set the standard for barmy goalkeepers. He enjoyed juggling the ball at his feet in front of his own goal – a trick later copied by Fabien Barthez to the detriment of Sir Alex Ferguson's blood pressure – and he also demonstrated a nonchalant penalty-saving technique that inspired Bruce Grobbelaar. In the 1978 group match against Scotland, Quiroga calmly stood there with his hands on his hips as Don Masson ran up to take a sixty-second-minute penalty. Then, at the last moment, he sprang into action, coming so far off his line that he was almost in the opposition half again and plunging to his right to save. If Masson had scored, Scotland would have taken a 2–1 lead and the outcome of their disastrous World Cup campaign might have been very different. In fact, Mel Gibson might have starred in a film about Ally MacLeod rather than William Wallace, and Willie Johnston might have received a year's free supply of hay-fever tablets from a grateful Scottish public. Quiroga had a lot to answer for.

An equally colourful character was Mexican keeper Jorge Campos, whose neon goalkeeping outfits were often more dazzling than his displays between the posts. In his fluorescent orange or lime green he looked more like a member of a motorway maintenance team than a World Cup side. Trinny and Susannah would surely have recommended downgrading to beige. Campos was Mexico's first choice at both the 1994 and 1998 finals, and he won 129 caps in total, but it was at club level that he was at his most outrageous. There, he might start in goal initially, but if the game needed rescuing, he would change shirt and switch to attack while a substitute donned the goalkeeping gloves. By such methods the versatile Campos scored thirty-five career goals, including fourteen in the 1989–90 season.

Then there was René Higuita, the wild Colombian goalkeeper for whom extra time meant a few weeks added to his prison sentence. He spent four months in jail in 1993 on suspicion of being involved in a drug cartel kidnapping (yes, it's hard to imagine such a thing going on in Colombia), before eventually being released without charge. In another scandal he tested positive for cocaine in 2004 while playing in Ecuador. Higuita was another Latino goalkeeper who liked to go on walkabout, but such risky methods backfired somewhat at the 1990 World Cup when, in the second-round match with Cameroon, he tried to

*Don't try this at home or away: René Higuita's amazing 'scorpion save'
at Wembley.*

dribble around Roger Milla 40 yards from goal, only for Milla to
dispossess him and shoot into the empty net. The goal put Colombia
out of the World Cup. In view of what happened to Andrés Escobar,
the Colombian player whose far less obvious blunder saw the
country eliminated from the 1994 tournament, Higuita could
consider himself lucky to be alive. By contrast, Higuita's finest hour
came at Wembley during a 1995 friendly when he introduced the
'scorpion save' to a disbelieving world. Jamie Redknapp's drive
warranted little more than a routine stop, but instead Higuita did a
handstand, arched his back and knocked the ball off the goal line
with the studs of his upturned boots. Of course, if David Seaman
had tried it he would have got them caught in his ponytail.

COME OFF IT, EILEEN

There is a school of thought that says that managers should be
forbidden from saying 'at the end of the day' unless it is actually

midnight. So why do they keep doing it? They expect fans to believe that they are great tactical innovators, yet in interviews they invariably trot out a stream of tired old clichés. Most managers seem to have their pet phrases or words that they use as a comfort blanket when faced by hostile journalists. With Sir Alf Ramsey it was 'most certainly', Graham Taylor became synonymous with 'do I not like that?', Sir Alex Ferguson's is thought to be 'bollocks to the BBC', while Glenn Hoddle has been known to favour 'at this moment in time' and 'situation'. Ironically, it was when Hoddle started to confuse his moments in time and talk about reincarnation that he found himself in an untenable situation. Reincarnation is a perfectly valid topic for discussion, but not when you're supposed to be talking about football. After all, you don't hear Lee Dixon and Gary Pallister slipping it into the conversation on *Score Interactive* on a Saturday afternoon just as Bolton have had a penalty appeal turned down. And apart from 'unbelievable comeback', Alan Hansen has yet to work reincarnation into a *Match of the Day* analysis. Mark Lawrenson has also kept quiet on the subject on *Football Focus*, possibly because he was a bloodhound in a former life and knows he's not really allowed on the sofa. By the time Hoddle's views on reincarnation became public, his star was already on the wane following an indifferent France '98, an ill-advised World Cup diary, and, perhaps most damaging of all, his bizarre relationship with Harlow pub landlady turned faith healer Eileen Drewery.

They first met back in 1976 when Hoddle, then a seventeen-year-old prodigy with Spurs, was dating Drewery's daughter Michelle. One day he hobbled round to Michelle's house, expecting nothing more from her mum than a cup of tea and maybe a chocolate digestive. Instead she offered psychic help to cure his torn leg muscle. At a time when a trainer's cold sponge could supposedly cure everything from cramp to a broken leg, and alternative therapies in football had not progressed much beyond 'eye of newt and wart of toad', Hoddle was unsurprisingly shocked by the suggestion and left in haste. Not to be thwarted in her efforts to help the young footballer, the resourceful Eileen opted for what she called remote

SHITE FACT

A giant brothel is opening just yards from the main stadium in Berlin to cater for fans at the 2006 World Cup. Its owner believes the three-storey Artemis brothel will be a big hit with World Cup visitors, having stated with authority that: 'Football and sex go together extremely well.'

access or 'distance' healing, and miraculously cleared up his injuries. Hoddle was impressed. He remembered the TV series *The Champions*, where, like Eileen, the three agents had special powers, and recalled that once, a long time ago, Spurs were champions. Clearly there was a link. Was Eileen really Sharron Macready in a barmaid's apron? Then, while holidaying in Israel in 1986, Glenn Hoddle found God, which to Jasper Carrott's way of thinking 'must have been one hell of a pass'.

As a born-again Christian, he explained to Eileen 'the wonderful feeling of peace' he had discovered, whereupon she confessed that her healing powers also came from God. She said she had used 'the channelled energy of God' to bring her husband Phil back from the jaws of death on three separate occasions. Bringing Spurs back from the dead, however, was too great a challenge even for the combined efforts of Eileen Drewery and the Almighty.

By now Eileen had given up pulling pints and was offering her services to the man in the street. Hoddle had become a firm disciple and when he was appointed England manager, he took steps to introduce her into the national set-up as an adviser. With a sceptical press unable to envisage how a faith healer would fit into a 4–4–2 system, he maintained that she was more of an agony aunt, providing counselling for troubled players. She had no shortage of ready-made clients. Paul Merson consulted her in his battle against drink and drugs, while

Gazza's case notes would have filled the British Library. Even those who doubted her effectiveness decided to call on her for fear that they might otherwise be omitted from future England teams. England had become the God squad and rumours were rife that Mrs D was now instrumental in team selection. As other football associations also began to consider the possibility of hiring people with special powers, the hot tip to become the new German national coach was Russell Grant. Meanwhile, the queue of male callers to Eileen's door grew so long that the Vice Squad might have taken an interest. Darren 'Sicknote' Anderton, a player so prone to injury that physios put a screen around him whenever he fell, described his consultation as beneficial. Robbie Fowler was less impressed, saying he spent his visit watching television with Mr Drewery. And unfortunately her powers of spiritual guidance did not extend to enabling David Batty to take a decent penalty.

Those who felt that Eileen was a) getting above her station or b) living on another planet were provided with further ammunition following England's final qualifying game for the 1998 World Cup. Needing only a draw in Rome to reach the finals, England achieved exactly that, even though they nearly snatched victory in the closing minutes when Ian Wright hit the post with the goal gaping. Eileen subsequently revealed that, with a little help from God, she had made Wright aim at the post rather than score for fear that a goal would spark crowd trouble! The men in white coats were on high alert.

HE SAID WHAT?

'They're not so different. They've got two arms and two legs and some of them even have heads.'

Australia manager Frank Arok on World Cup qualifying opponents, Scotland, in 1985

SHITE FACT

Iran's players prepared for their opening group match with Yugoslavia at the 1998 World Cup by taking part in a three-hour mourning session in memory of a seventh-century saint. The players beat their chests and wept together until midnight while a teacher recounted the saint's death. They lost 1–0 the following day.

During the build-up to the World Cup finals, Hoddle expressed the view that young Michael Owen was 'not a natural goalscorer'. Yet when Owen was introduced to the action, he was comfortably England's sharpest forward through a stuttering group campaign. Defeat to Romania had given England a second-round clash with old rivals Argentina. Again Owen shone by winning a penalty and scoring a spectacular goal, only for England (minus Beckham, banished for taking a kick at Diego Simeone) to bow out on penalties after Paul Ince and David Batty had their spot-kicks saved. It was the first penalty Batty had ever taken in a competitive match . . . and it showed. Frankly, Norah Batty could have done better.

England's bold showing against Argentina had earned Hoddle a brief respite from the assassins of Fleet Street, but then he made the mistake of publishing his World Cup diary, in which he revealed that a drunken Gazza had gone berserk on learning that he hadn't been included in the squad for France. Apparently he had smashed a lamp in Hoddle's hotel room and kicked a chair, although the chest of drawers was a bit too quick for him. Hoddle also devoted half a dozen pages to the merits of Mrs Drewery and stated that his one big mistake had been in not taking her to France. The general consensus of opinion was that he had made a far bigger mistake in not practising penalties. Hoddle's reliance on his faith-healer friend was now making him a laughing stock and he came under further fire when it emerged that he and Eileen planned to open a fee-paying spiritual sanctuary. Tony Adams was pleased because he thought it was a donkey sanctuary.

In an attempt to repair the England manager's increasingly fragile relations with the press, the FA embarked on a charm offensive ahead of a 1999 friendly with France. But in an interview with *The Times* in February, Hoddle ended up talking about reincarnation and was quoted as saying: 'You and I have been physically given two hands and two legs and half-decent brains. Some people have not been born like that for a reason. The karma is working from another lifetime . . . What you sow, you have to reap. You have to look at things that happened in your life and ask why. It comes around.' Hoddle's comments, interpreted as suggesting that disabled people are being punished for sins in a former life, caused a predictable uproar. The matter was so serious it was even debated on that heavyweight political platform, *This Morning With Richard and Judy*. Meanwhile, Sports Minister Tony Banks said of Hoddle: 'If his theory is correct, he is in for real problems in the next life. He will probably be doomed to come back as Glenn Hoddle!' With only Eileen loyally defending his corner, Hoddle fought back in an interview with ITN, which demonstrated that whatever sins he may have been guilty of, an overbearing intellect was not one of them. In it he said: 'The only reason people are saying I should resign is that they are saying I have come out and said that people disabled and handicapped have been paying for their sins and I have never ever said that. I don't believe that. At this moment in time, if that changes in years to come I don't know, but what happens here today and changes as we go along, that is part of life's learning and part of your inner beliefs. But at this moment in time I did not say them things.' The FA were not impressed, however, and asked Hoddle to pack his clichés. Eileen Drewery's spell as England's spiritual guru – the Maharishi of Harlow – was over. After Kevin Keegan's short reign, the FA decided to avoid further scandals by appointing a quiet, upstanding Swede. What a shrewd move that turned out to be . . .

SHITE FACT

After Brazil crushed Italy 4–1 in the 1970 final, jubilant fans mobbed the players so enthusiastically that one of the Brazilian stars, Roberto Rivelino, collapsed under the weight of the celebrations and had to be carried to the dressing room on a stretcher.

THE OLDEST SWINGER IN TOWN

In an all-time country and western XI, Dolly Parton would obviously be centre forward, Jim Reeves would go flying down the wing (until he crashed into the advertising boards), and Tammy Wynette would do a close-marking job so that she could stand by her man. As for the sub, it would have to be Roger Miller, quite possibly the only country singer to share a name with a World Cup hero. The link may be tenuous and contrived (OK, the link *is* tenuous and contrived), but Cameroon star Roger Milla was actually born Roger Miller before changing his surname so that it sounded more African. Milla was the first African to play in three World Cup finals tournaments, and in 1994 he established a record that may never be broken, by becoming, at the ripe old age of forty-two years and thirty-nine days, the oldest goalscorer in the finals. And when he celebrated with the Makossa – that crazy little dance he always did around the corner flag – the world smiled. He could have looked the most embarrassing thing to hit the dance floor since Prince Charles, but he turned out to be the oldest swinger in town.

Milla played most of his club football in France and made his international debut in 1978. Four years later he was part of the Cameroon side that reached the World Cup finals. He had a seemingly good goal ruled out against Peru, but three draws from their three group games were not enough to send 'the

*Old snake hips Roger Milla turned pole dancing into a spectator
sport for footballers.*

Indomitable Lions' into the second round. His club form had been erratic until, in 1984, he signed for Saint-Etienne, and went on to score twenty-two goals in thirty-one appearances. Continuing to improve with age, he was voted Player of the Tournament at the 1986 African Cup of Nations before announcing his retirement from international football the following year. Two testimonial matches drew nearly 100,000 fans, following which he moved to Réunion, an island in the Indian Ocean, for what he thought would be a quiet retirement. But like an office worker who has a leaving-do with lots of presents and then rejoins the company the following week, Milla was about to make an incredible comeback . . . only on this occasion nobody asked for their toaster back. It wasn't even his decision. Out of the blue he received a phone call from the President of Cameroon begging him to come out of retirement and help the national team at the 1990 World Cup. It was an invitation he could hardly refuse and, used largely as a second-half substitute to preserve his ageing legs, he scored four times to help Cameroon to the quarter-finals where they lost narrowly to England. And he celebrated each goal by performing the sort of hip-swivelling routine with a corner flag that punters pay good money for at Spearmint Rhino. His bursts of pace, his mazy runs and an enthusiasm that made Bonnie Langford look positively apathetic by comparison, endeared him to the watching millions and made Milla a household name.

That should have been the end of his World Cup story as once more he retired, but when Cameroon qualified for the 1994 finals, he returned to the ranks yet again. By now he was officially forty-two, although one member of the Cameroon delegation told journalists that Milla was actually forty-six! Sadly, the fairy-tale ending was hijacked by a big bad wolf named Oleg Salenko who scored five times as Russia sent Cameroon crashing out of the tournament. However, Milla, coming on as a sub, did net Cameroon's consolation goal and in the process wrote himself into the record books. He is currently enjoying his third retirement but, in view of the fact that football really is a funny old game, only a fool would bet against Roger Milla reappearing at the 2014 World Cup and becoming the first goalscorer to possess a bus pass. And just watch him do that celebratory dance around his Zimmer frame.

BARMY ARMIES

For football fans the World Cup has always been a special occasion. For German fans there is a chance to visit some of the countries they missed out on in 1939; for English fans it is an opportunity to collect continental ASBOs; and for Welsh fans the World Cup finals are a once-in-a-lifetime experience – provided they live to at least eighty. Thankfully amid the baton charging, bar brawls and provocative posturing that have all too often turned the World Cup finals into a cross between *It's a Knockout* and *The Sweeney*, there are still one or two supporter stories to gladden the heart.

So let's hear it for Emil Holliger, a forty-eight-year-old Swiss window-cleaner, who, in June 1966, announced his intention to push a pram, decked with national colours and cowbells, across Europe to Sheffield where Switzerland were due to meet West Germany in their opening tie at that summer's World Cup.

Then, in May 1986, fifty-two-year-old Argentine fan Pedro Gatica set off from his home in Buenos Aires and cycled all the way to Mexico for the World Cup. After pedalling for nearly five thousand miles along roads of varying quality, he finally arrived in Mexico, only to discover to his horror that he couldn't afford to buy a ticket. Worse still, while he haggled over the price of entry, thieves stole his bike!

But for sheer commitment it is hard to match Ken Baily, who, from 1970 until his death in 1993, was the official mascot of the England team. Sporting his familiar red tailcoat, white gloves, Union Jack waistcoat, either a top hat or a white pith helmet, and brandishing a rattle, this eccentric John Bull figure started out as mascot for his hometown club Bournemouth in the 1950s, before

England mascot Ken Baily made a prat of himself in over forty countries.

earning his international call-up. He proved a colourful addition to the ranks at the 1966 World Cup and his efforts were even recognized by Subbuteo who produced a figure of him standing in full dress with his arms aloft waving a rattle, which was given away to fans at the England–Portugal game in 1969. A throwback to the days of jumpers for goalposts, his presence seemed incongruous with the modern game. Despite being mercilessly taunted by the less savoury England fans, Ken carried on regardless, his official status allowing him to make a prat of himself in over forty countries. Yet curiously his most famous moment occurred on the rugby field when he used his Union Jack flag to conceal streaker Erica Roe's 40-inch chest at Twickenham in January 1982. Ken Baily always was out of touch with what the public wanted.

SHITE FACT

Nigerian fans went on a three-day fast before the 2002 finals in an attempt to secure divine intervention to help the team. Despite their best efforts, though, Nigeria finished bottom of their group with just one point.

WORLD CUP MASCOTS

The prevailing feeling in FIFA seems to be that all of the World Cup's ills will be eliminated automatically if each tournament has its own cute mascot. The divers, the spitters, the cloggers – they will all think twice when they remember they are being watched by a worldwide audience of millions and a smiling orange. Since that cheeky little British lion World Cup Willie strutted his stuff in 1966, there have been a succession of cheesy mascots, coming full circle this summer with another lion, the proud Goleo VI, and his sidekick Pille, a talking football. At least the 2006 choice draws on FIFA's area of expertise because talking balls is what they're good at. Here is the full list of World Cup mascots:

1966 – World Cup Willie: a pugnacious lion with a Beatle haircut wearing a Union Jack shirt.

1970 – Juanito: a small Mexican boy in an ill-fitting sombrero.

1974 – Tip and Tap: two German boys (one dark, one fair) bursting for a game of football.

1978 – Gauchito: yet another cute little mite, this time from Argentina.

1982 – Naranjito: a Spanish orange with a maniacal grin; think Jim Rosenthal after too long under the sun lamp.

1986 – Pique: a moustachioed Mexican chilli pepper – you don't get many of those to the pound.

1990 – Ciao: an Italian cuboid stickman straight from a Rubik's puzzle; it was supposed to represent a footballer, but ended up looking more like an anorexic Bertie Bassett.

1994 – Striker: the American dog bore an uncanny resemblance to Huckleberry Hound.

1998 – Footix: the blue French cockerel has probably been destroyed since the bird flu scare.

2002 – Ato, Nik and Kaz: the Spheriks, as they were known, apparently represented energy particles in the atmosphere and were chosen after a vote by soccer fans in Japan and Korea; they were designed to show the fun side of nuclear physics.

2006 – Goleo VI and Pille: a lion king with a football that speaks – Germany's answer to Morecambe and Wise.

SHITE FACT

The 1930 final between Argentina and Uruguay was preceded by a squabble over which ball to use. As the two teams were unable to agree, it was eventually decided that the first half should be played with Argentina's ball and the second half with Uruguay's. Trailing by two goals to one at half-time after playing with their opponent's football, Uruguay embraced their own ball in the second half and ended the game as 4–2 winners.

WHO'S YOUR FATHER, REFEREE?

PREMATURE EJECTION

The referees at the 2002 World Cup finals were thought by some to have been the best that Korean money could buy. Such accusations were probably unfounded, not least because to be chosen to officiate at a World Cup tournament represents the pinnacle of a referee's career. Only the *crème de la crème* are afforded such an honour – i.e. those who can trace their ancestry back to their father, have most of their mental faculties intact (unless it's a full moon) and possess some vision in one eye. The seeds for refereeing incompetence were sown at the very first World Cup where a South American proved himself to be the worst timekeeper since Ethelred the Unready.

Gilberto de Almeida Rego of Brazil was put in charge of the Pool One game between strongly fancied Argentina and France. To the delight of the partisan Uruguayan crowd, the Argentines were still struggling to make the vital breakthrough as the game entered the last ten minutes. But then Luis Monti, who had single-handedly crippled at least three of the French team in a manner that made Peter Storey look like Julie Andrews, scored from a quickly taken free kick. Bravely, France tried to fight back and when winger Marcel Langiller ran the length of the field, an equalizer seemed inevitable. However, just as Langiller was about to pull the trigger, referee Rego blew for full time . . . six minutes early. While the relieved Argentines celebrated wildly, the French camp surrounded Senhor Rego and, amid much arm-waving, informed him of his blunder. The referee was persuaded to consult his watch, which read four minutes past Mickey Mouse's right hand. He quickly realized that he had blown for time after playing just eighty-four minutes. Apologizing profusely and insisting that it was an error made in good faith, he told the disbelieving Argentines that there were still another six minutes to play. The Argentine inside left, Cierro, was so shaken by the news that he fainted. The match duly restarted, but the delay had robbed the French of their momentum and the final minutes passed without further incident. Before his next appointment, the Brazilian referee not only brushed up on the rules, but he also learned to tell the time.

BECKHAM'S DARKEST HOUR

'Dad,' said six-year-old Brooklyn Beckham. 'Will you help me with my maths homework?'

'I don't know, son,' said David. 'It wouldn't really be right, would it?'

'Probably not, Dad. But have a go anyway.'

Long before admitting that he struggled to do his son's maths homework (he thought an isosceles triangle was near Bermuda), David Beckham was being ridiculed for his alleged stupidity.

What do you do if David Beckham throws a pin at you? – Run, he's got a grenade in his mouth.

Why did David Beckham bury his driving licence? – Because it had expired.

What's the difference between David Beckham and a new Airfix model? – One's a glueless kit . . .

Why did David Beckham throw bread down the lavatory? – He wanted to feed the toilet duck.

It became a national pastime to poke fun at Becks and his wife Victoria (aka Posh Spice) for having more money than sense and for a lifestyle that inspired the whole *Footballers' Wives* phenomenon. When young Brooklyn told his parents he had to take a protractor to school, he is said to have turned up next day in a brand new Massey Ferguson. But there was a time when Beckham was public enemy number one. He couldn't have

Beckham went from hero to zero after being sent off against Argentina in 1998.

attracted more negative publicity if he and Victoria had been photographed staying at Saddam Hussein's holiday home. And it was all the result of events surrounding the 1998 World Cup.

In his younger days, Beckham had a decidedly dodgy temperament. He was easier to wind up than a Rolex. He had been told that opponents might try to get him sent off at France '98 but the warnings, no doubt like Victoria's singing, fell on deaf ears. The flashpoint was England's second-round game with Argentina, refereed by the Dane Kim Milton

Nielsen, a man who hid the ruthless efficiency of Adolf Hitler in the frame of Basil Fawlty. Nielsen was so tall that ice formed on his head during evening matches. Players rarely questioned his authority, not least because Paul Ince would have needed a stepladder to have an eyeball-to-eyeball confrontation. Two minutes into the second half, with the game evenly balanced at 2–2, Beckham was brought down from behind by Diego Simeone. As he lay on the ground, Beckham aimed a sly, petulant kick at the Argentine . . . right under the referee's nose. There was nothing vicious in it, but Beckham was instantly banished from the pitch and with him went England's hopes. After his team's eventual defeat on penalties, a chastened Beckham apologized profusely, calling his sending-off 'the worst moment of my career' and adding, 'I want every England supporter to know how deeply sorry I am.'

Sadly, mindless morons running amok in provincial towns following an exit from a major tournament has become almost as much of an English tradition as dancing around the maypole, and the public were not prepared to forgive and forget. A radio poll in Manchester revealed that 61 per cent of listeners never wanted to see Beckham play for England again, an effigy of him was hung outside a London pub, and the *Daily Mirror* printed a dartboard with a picture of Beckham in the middle so that fans could take out their frustrations on their fallen hero in the privacy of their own homes. And these were the same people that were labelling Beckham immature. Meanwhile, lucrative sponsorship deals were put on hold and it seemed that the Boy David might be hounded out of the country before an unlikely saviour appeared in the form of the Archbishop of Canterbury, Dr George Carey, who led calls for him to be forgiven. The whole unsavoury episode was eventually forgotten, except by pub jokers who had been presented with a dubious new range of Beckham material. What's the difference between Posh and Becks? – Posh doesn't kick back when she's taken from behind.

SHITE FACT

After Swiss referee Kurt Rothlisberger admitted his error in failing to award Belgium a penalty in their second-round match with Germany at the 1994 finals, FIFA dropped him for the rest of the tournament.

THE REF WHO PAID THE PENALTY

A referee can usually count his friends on one finger of one hand – which coincidentally is how his critics often express their opinion of him. But at least most of our men in black have some vague grasp of the laws of the game, which is more than can be said for Toshimitsu Yoshida, the Japanese official in charge of a 2005 World Cup qualifier between Uzbekistan and Bahrain. His performance was so inept that the Asian Football Confederation suspended him indefinitely. The first leg of the tie took place in Tashkent in early September, and the Uzbekistani hosts were leading 1–0 when Mr Yoshida awarded them a penalty in the thirty-eighth minute. The spot kick was duly converted by Server Djeparov, only for the referee to disallow the goal because he had noticed another Uzbekistan player encroaching in the penalty area while the ball was being kicked. Under Law 14 he should have ordered the penalty to be retaken, but instead he decided to punish the offence by awarding Bahrain a free kick! Uzbekistan's English manager Bobby Houghton protested to the fourth official at the time of the incident, but apparently the latter did not discuss it with Mr Yoshida until half-time, by which time it was too late.

Uzbekistan went on to win 1–0 but, with the second leg in Bahrain still to come, they were not happy with their slender advantage. Officials of the Uzbekistan Football Federation protested to FIFA about Mr Yoshida's blunder and also over the fact that Bahrain's Mohammed Jumaa Abdulla was not sent off for the handball that led to the penalty. They demanded to be awarded the match 3–0. Unfortunately, FIFA had other ideas, and ruled that because the referee had committed a grave technical error, the result was void. They ordered that the match should be replayed the following month. Unsurprisingly, Uzbekistan were livid. 'The referee stole our second goal and now FIFA is stealing our first goal,' complained Alisher Nikimbaev, the head of international relations for the Uzbekistan Football Federation (UFF). 'Now we must start the first match from 0–0 in the first minute. It's not fair for our team.' It was pretty brave of FIFA to take on an outfit calling themselves the UFF, but they stood firm, rejecting further Uzbekistan claims that, if the match had to be replayed, it should at least start from the thirty-eighth minute penalty with a 1–0 lead awarded to the aggrieved party. Almost inevitably the wronged Uzbekistan players were less effective in the replay and could only manage a 1–1 draw. And when the second leg ended 0–0, it was Bahrain who went through on the away goals rule. The difference was that this time there was no Mr Yoshida on hand to apply his own unique interpretation of the rule.

SHITE FACT

Despite being shown a second yellow card in a first-round game against Chile in June 1974, Australia's Ray Richards was allowed to stay on the pitch by Iranian referee Jafar Namdar until the reserve official pointed out the oversight to a linesman four minutes later.

HE SAID WHAT?

'We're the champions of Africa, what are you? Italy is world famous for the Mafia and Fiat, not for football.'

Samson Emeka Omeruah, president of the Nigerian Football Federation, winding up Italian journalists before their second-round meeting in July 1994, which Italy won 2–1

BY THE BOOK

Few sportsmen have revelled in their nickname quite as much as Welsh referee Clive 'The Book' Thomas. At a time when the likes of Gordon Hill, Tommy Dawes and Roger Kirkpatrick officiated matches with a ready smile, Thomas was the Simon Cowell of the referees' panel – the Mr Nasty who invariably found himself the centre of attention in someone else's show and who wasn't the slightest bit worried about upsetting people. A stickler for the letter of the law, he applied the rules with the same zeal as the head of the Spanish Inquisition. As someone who once booked a player being stretchered off with a broken leg, you suspected that not even the last rites would prevent Clive Thomas issuing a caution. He actively seemed to encourage his notoriety, perhaps reasoning that the publicity would help him reach the top of his profession. And being Welsh he had an unfair advantage over other British referees hoping to officiate at the World Cup finals because he knew that he would always be neutral.

So it was that Thomas came to referee the Group Three match between Brazil and Sweden at the 1978 finals. The score was 1–1 when Brazil were awarded a corner with seconds remaining. The corner was swung over and Zico powered an unstoppable header into the net for what looked like a last-gasp winner. The Brazilians celebrated wildly, the Swedes looked crestfallen until they noticed that Mr Thomas was signalling that he had disallowed the goal – not for any infringement, but because he had blown for full time while the ball was in the air. He was of course perfectly entitled to do so, but common sense dictates that you don't blow the final whistle just as the ball is about to enter the net. Leaving the field under a hail of coins, he imperiously brushed aside all Brazilian protests. The Welshman was not for turning. Amid the furore that followed, the Swedes tried to claim that as the corner came over they had relaxed when they heard the final whistle, but nobody really believed them. As an excuse it was no more plausible than Charles Kennedy claiming, 'It was only a soft drink.' Thomas's performance failed to impress his FIFA bosses not because of the disallowed goal, but because he had covered his face theatrically with his hands when Sweden nearly scored an own goal. Ironically, the man who was so intent on playing it by the book was now being discarded for becoming a personality referee. And in the grey world of FIFA that would never do.

In what was surely the most frightening news to come out of Wales since Max Boyce went into the studio to record a new album, Treorchy's most famous referee was appointed High Sheriff of Mid Glamorgan in 2005. Rigorous clampdowns were expected on everything from out-of-tune male voice choirs to overdue library books. Zero tolerance had come to the Rhondda Valley.

SHITE FACT

The 1994 World Cup qualifying tie between Angola and Egypt in Luanda was postponed after the referee failed to turn up.

FIVE MEMORABLE GOAL CELEBRATIONS

The days when the scoring of a goal was greeted by a firm handshake and a 'well done, old boy' have long been consigned to history. First, the celebrations graduated to hugs, then kissing, and now goals are marked by increasingly elaborate routines or acrobatic displays. With his money, Roman Abramovich (or Ronan O'Bramovic as he is known in Dublin) will probably hire the Red Arrows to fly over when Chelsea score their first goal of the new season. Of course, Sunderland might have the best goal celebration of all, but nobody would ever know. We've already examined Roger Milla's exhibition of dirty dancing with the corner flag, but here are five more World Cup celebrations that stick in the mind:

The Republic of Ireland's Robbie Keane marked his goal against Saudi Arabia in 2002 with his usual series of cartwheels, but followed it by firing an imaginary bow and arrow instead of the more familiar gunslinger routine. Was he trying to indicate that, in the absence of namesake Roy, Ireland had more than one string to their bow? At any rate, by popular demand, the gunslinger has since returned.

SHITE FACT

Dutch referee Laurens van Ravens took the decision to start the second half of the West Germany–Morocco group match at Mexico 1970 while the Moroccans were still strolling back on to the pitch. As a result, Moroccan goalkeeper Allal Ben Kassu had to sprint across his penalty area to save a German shot as it was heading for the empty net.

Julius Aghahowa refused to let his status as a professional footballer get in the way of his gymnastic aspirations.

After scoring a superlative last-minute goal to defeat Argentina in the quarter-finals in 1998, Holland's Dennis Bergkamp looked up towards the heavens with his arms in the air before falling flat on his back, his arms still pointing skywards. The symbolic pointing to the sky was seen by many as being a thank you to God, but Bergkamp might also have been saying: 'You'll never get me up in one of those things.'

When Papa Bouba Diop scored Senegal's shock winner against France in 2002, he threw his shirt down and the rest of the team danced around it. The routine was vaguely reminiscent of Pan's People dancing to a Bay City Rollers hit.

Julius Aghahowa of Nigeria performed seven successive somer-saults following his goal against Sweden at the 2002 finals, making Rob Earnshaw's couple of somersaults look as bland as an Alan Shearer goal celebration. Though high on technical merit, it is surely low on common sense, as one day such a celebration might result in six months on the treatment table for the agile Aghahowa.

A few days after his wife had given birth to their third child, Brazil's Bebeto scored against Holland in the 1994 quarter-finals. He celebrated the goal by running over to the touchline and rocking an imaginary baby, joined on either side by team-mates Mazinho and Romário copying the movement. Beautifully choreographed, it could have brought a tear to a glass eye.

Bebeto (centre) leads the Brazilian baby rockers in 1994. They scored a 5.7 for artistic impression.

POLITICAL INTERFERENCE

A PRINCE AMONG MEN

Money doesn't just talk in Kuwait, it positively screams. So when the national team qualified for the 1982 World Cup finals, the entire squad were handsomely rewarded with speedboats. It was just like being on *Bullseye*. As the brother of the country's ruler and president of the Kuwaiti Football Association, Prince Fahd knew the power of money better than most. He also had more of it to wave about than most. Back home his word was final and he probably saw no reason why it should be a different ball game at the World Cup. His was very much the Robert Maxwell approach to football.

After earning a creditable 1–1 draw against Czechoslovakia in their opening fixture, Kuwait's next opponents were the emerging French in Valladolid. Boasting such silky smooth midfielders as Michel Platini, Jean Tigana and Alain Giresse, France were expected to make a bold show in Spain but had been rocked by a 3–1 defeat to England. Needing a win to get back on track, they

SHITE FACT

To mark Zaire's appearance in the 1974 finals – the first by a black African country – President Mobutu promised each member of the squad a house, a car and a holiday. But when the team lost all three games without scoring a goal, the generous offer was abruptly withdrawn.

Before crossing swords with Kuwaiti royalty, referee Miroslav Stupar tosses what turns out to be a most unlucky coin.

pounded the Kuwaitis mercilessly and led 3–0 shortly after half-time. Kuwait managed to pull one back through Abdullah Al-Buloushi, but the result was seemingly put beyond doubt when Giresse restored the three-goal advantage. However, the Kuwaitis immediately surrounded Russian referee Miroslav Stupar and protested about the validity of the goal, saying that they had stopped playing after hearing a whistle from the crowd. Up in the stand, the prince looked on aghast at the injustice unfolding before his eyes and with a regal wave of his hand, called his players from the field.

While the prince, his robes flowing grandly, made his way down to the touchline, the Kuwaiti team continued to remonstrate with the referee via the international language of dissent. It seemed that they were ready to return to the dressing room and forfeit the game until the prince apparently struck a deal with the referee. The game could continue but only on condition that the referee reversed his original decision and disallowed the French goal. Confronted by the prince in full ceremonial bluster, Mr Stupar was no more assertive than *Dad's Army*'s Private Godfrey in the face of a German Panzer division. He meekly acceded to this unprecedented demand and restarted the game at 3–1 with a bounce-up. Fortunately the end result was not affected by Mr Stupar's inexplicable change of heart and Maxime Bossis scored late on to give France their 4–1 victory. Prince Fahd was subsequently rapped over the knuckles by FIFA for his intervention, although the £8,000 fine amounted to little more than loose change, and Mr Stupar was quietly dropped from the tournament. His indecision was final.

HE SAID WHAT?

'Make love before matches? My lads can do as they like, but it's not advisable at half-time.'

German coach Berti Vogts at the 1998 World Cup, showing the sense of humour he would later need for the Scotland job

ALL THE KING'S MEN

Imagine if the Queen were to inform Brian Barwick that *she* wanted to pick the team for the 2006 World Cup. There would be uproar, not least because Her Majesty is known to favour a 3–5–2 system with wing backs. While the prospect of having a grandmother in charge of the team might well put a glint in Wayne Rooney's eye, there would be concerns that she might invoke a clause in the constitution that promises a game to the heir to the throne. Thus Prince Charles tried to allay fears that he was out of touch with the modern game by revealing how much he was looking forward to teaming up with Tom Finney. Curiously there is actually a precedent for a monarch choosing the national side. Back in 1930, when FIFA were organizing the inaugural World Cup, the Romanian Football Association initially declined the invitation to send a team to Uruguay but, barely a month before the tournament was due to begin, King Carol II came to the throne. The sporty monarch, whose previous knowledge of international affairs amounted to bedding every princess in Europe, immediately set to work on Romania's entry, paving the way by granting an amnesty to all of the country's suspended players. He then picked the team himself and coerced the companies that employed the players into giving them three months' paid leave. In the event, they didn't need that long. After just two games – the second a 4–0 hammering by the host nation – the king's men were boarding the boat home. And the king went back to what he did best – chasing women.

SHITE FACT

Angered by the national team's elimination from the qualifying rounds of the 1998 World Cup, the King of Algeria banned the coach and his assistant from working in football for life and also dissolved the National League.

THE BOTTOM OF THE BARREL

TWO DAYS OF TORTURE

The godfather of football on the Pacific island of Guam is Charlie Whang, who once scored five goals in a game at the age of fifty-eight. Even as a sprightly eighty-year-old, he was still playing football with the island's youngsters, and many consider him unlucky not to have earned a place in Guam's first ever World Cup line-up in 2000. But perhaps the saying that there is no substitute for experience is something of a myth. Certainly Guam's manager decreed that, in Charlie's case, the ability to run more than ten yards without needing a lie-down was a good substitute for experience. Lacking Charlie's old head and equally old legs, Guam, ranked 200th in the world (ahead of only Montserrat and American Samoa), travelled to Iran in November 2000, where they made their World Cup debut in a qualifying match.

Confidence was at a premium, especially as Iran had a history of being ruthless with island upstarts, having thrashed the Maldives 17–0 in the qualifying tournament for the 1998 finals. That score was a World Cup record at the time, so Guam now hoped Iran were feeling generous. However, generosity in Iran can be in shorter supply than sand in Greenland and Guam were duly brushed aside 19–0. At this point, with just one game to play, it would be fair to say that Guam did not hold out much hope of qualifying from Asia Group Two, particularly if it came down to goal difference. Nevertheless, two days later they fulfilled their second fixture – against Tajikistan – looking for some improvement. And they got it, this time losing only 16–0. Having conceded thirty-five goals in the space of forty-eight hours, Guam's World Cup dream was over for another four years. Charlie Whang was still waiting for his call-up.

SHITE FACT

San Marino failed to score in any of their eight qualifying matches for France '98, conceding forty-two goals in the process. They were so poor that even Wales beat them twice.

SLAUGHTER OF THE SAMOANS

Any nation that has been managed by Terry Venables in the past has inevitably endured more than its fair share of disappointment. But Australia put those sad times behind them in April 2001 when, in the space of two days, they totalled fifty-three goals without reply in two World Cup qualifying ties. And that was fielding a weakened team, minus English-based stars such as Lucas Neill, Harry Kewell and Mark Viduka who were all unavailable. First, Frank Farina's side thrashed Tonga 22–0 to set a new World Cup record, but that was really just a warm-up for their meeting with American Samoa at Coffs Harbour, New South Wales.

In the light of what had happened to Tonga, the American Samoans could have been forgiven for staying at home. After all, they were ranked 203rd in the world (the lowest possible ranking) and current form indicated that they were considerably worse than Tonga. The qualifying rounds had been a nightmare from the start for American Samoa's manager Tony Langkilde who discovered that nearly all of his original squad were ineligible because they didn't possess US passports. Now, facing the relative might of Australia, he couldn't even call upon the services of his under-20 team because they were all busy revising for exams. So he had to field a fifteen-year-old in a team with an average age of just nineteen. Nor were their preparations exactly ideal, as they had to buy their strip and

THEY THINK IT'S ALL SHITE . . . IT IS NOW!

boots from a local supermarket. Somehow it's hard to picture José Mourinho having to pop into the nearest Asda and buy the Chelsea kit for that afternoon's match. No wonder coach Tunoa Lui admitted to seeking divine intervention before the Australia game.

He was right to be concerned. After holding the Australians at bay for the first eight minutes, American Samoa's keeper Nicky Salapu was beaten by an innocuous-looking cross-cum-shot from Con Boutsianis. A mere fifteen minutes later, American Samoa

A North Sea fisherman spent less time picking things out of the net than American Samoa keeper Nicky Salapu.

were 8–0 down. By half-time, with the shell-shocked Salapu having to deal with a barrage of shots from all angles, the score had risen to 16–0. Even the most optimistic manager would have fought shy of saying, 'We can turn this around in the second half, lads,' so one suspects that Langkilde's interval pep talk was more along the lines of keeping your discipline, not letting your heads drop and taking your time retrieving the ball from the back of the net. A further eight goals in the first twenty-one minutes of the second half – including three in three minutes – maintained Australia's momentum before things went strangely quiet for twelve whole minutes. This lull seemed more a case of the Australians getting bored with scoring at will than of the American Samoans finally mastering the art of defending because it was followed by seven more goals in the last twelve minutes. The final score was 31–0 with Archie Thompson, winning only his third cap, netting a record thirteen. He claimed his first hat-trick after twenty-seven minutes, his second after thirty-seven, his third on fifty-six and his fourth on seventy-five minutes. David Zdrilic weighed in with eight while the Pacific islanders' solitary attack in the match came in the eighty-sixth minute, by which time they were already 29–0 down. The one consolation for American Samoa was that it could have been even worse. The official FIFA goal counter (who really earned his money on this occasion) originally calculated the final score as 32–0 until a discrepancy was spotted.

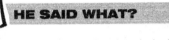

HE SAID WHAT?

'We are asking the Lord to help keep the score down.'

American Samoa coach Tunoa Lui before his team's record 31–0 drubbing by Australia in 2001

SHITE FACT

Jeered by fans following a disappointing draw with the Cape Verde Islands in a 2003 qualifying tie, Swaziland players suddenly lost their cool and ordered the driver to stop the team bus. They then leaped from the vehicle and, menacingly waving sticks, chased their tormentors down the road.

THE LONG WAIT

There are certain events that are notoriously poorly attended – the annual meeting of the Friends of Jens Lehmann, the Iain Dowie Lookalike Society, and of course the Mike Riley Appreciation Society. Add to these the Luxembourg Sports Personality of the Year Awards. You have to be a very special person to be a fan of the Luxembourg national football team. Very special and very patient. And given the size of their crowds, it probably also helps if you don't suffer from agoraphobia.

Luxembourg have entered the World Cup since 1934 and on every occasion they have finished bottom of their qualifying group, never even getting close to reaching the finals. Out of a total of ninety-one matches played, they have won just two, the last being over thirty years ago in 1972 when they somehow managed to defeat Turkey 2–0. The event probably still warrants a day of mourning in Istanbul. Luxembourg's golden years were in the 1960s when, apart from the odd nine-goal thumping by England, they recorded their only other World Cup success – 4–2 against Portugal in 1961. And after a surprise away win against Holland (who played as if they had clogs on back then), Luxembourg nearly reached the finals of the 1964 European Championships, only going out to Denmark in a play-off.

Following that epic win over Turkey, Luxembourg entered a

barren spell (a disaster for most countries, but a mere blip by Luxembourg standards), during which they suffered thirty-two successive World Cup defeats before snatching a shock 1–1 draw in Brussels in October 1989. The fact that Belgium, who had won 5–0 in Luxembourg a few months earlier, had already qualified for the finals as group winners perhaps explains why they felt charitable towards their neighbours. There were hopes that this draw might herald an upturn in Luxembourg's fortunes, but it proved a false dawn. The qualifying group for the 2006 World Cup saw them lose all twelve games, conceding forty-eight goals in the process. They showed a particular weakness down the right flank, thereby encouraging opposing managers to instruct their players to pass the Duchy on the left-hand side.

THE WORLD'S WORST TWO TEAMS

As the perfect antidote to the 2002 World Cup final, a Dutch documentary company conceived the idea of staging a match between the two worst national teams in the world. Thus a few hours before Brazil took on Germany in Japan, Bhutan and Montserrat, 202nd and 203rd in the FIFA rankings respectively, slugged it out in the tiny Changlimithang Stadium high in the Himalayas. Any similarity to the real thing was purely coincidental. There was no play-acting, no war of words between the managers, no sponsorship, no ticket touts, and no unpleasant chanting. Not once did the home fans refer to the 1995 volcano that rendered half of Montserrat uninhabitable and destroyed the national football stadium. Equally, the small Montserrat entourage refrained from singing any songs that mentioned the fact that the Bhutan national costume is the kilt.

For the Montserrat players, who included an artist and an MP, the journey to the Bhutan capital of Thimphu took five days, involving countless airline meals. Unsurprisingly seven of the team were struck down by food poisoning. It wasn't as if they had a large squad either. There are only 150 amateur players on the Caribbean island and the national league consists of just five teams, as a result of which nobody gets too excited about the Cup draw. And on arriving in Bhutan, the players had to adjust to the 7,500 feet altitude and a crowd of 20,000 (all of whom were admitted free), which was four times the entire population of Montserrat.

The odds appeared stacked in favour of Bhutan and so it proved. Watched by the country's full cabinet and under the eagle eye of English referee Steve Bennett, the Bhutan team set about capitalizing on the obvious nerves of Montserrat goalkeeper Cecil Lake. The jittery Lake could hardly blame the illness that was going around – even if he had caught the stomach bug he would probably have dropped it. After letting in a soft header from captain Wangyel Dorji to give Bhutan an early lead, in the second half Lake was beaten twice more by the Bhutan skipper and once by striker Dinesh Chhetri. The 4–0 defeat confirmed Montserrat as officially the worst national team in the world. With echoes of Alf Ramsey from Mexico 1970, their coach William Lewis blamed the result on the altitude. For their part, Bhutan hoped that the triumph would help propel them up the FIFA rankings. And by June 2005 they had reached the lofty heights of number 188. Brazil beware!

SHITE FACT

I don't believe it! During qualifying for the 1982 tournament, New Zealand goalkeeper Richard Wilson went 920 minutes without conceding a goal. Among New Zealand's victories en route to their first ever finals was a 13–0 hammering of Fiji in Auckland, which was a record World Cup score at the time.

SVEN'S ENGLAND DIARY

Sven-Göran Eriksson's secret diary of his five and a half years in charge of the England team is the most eagerly anticipated football book since *Glenn Hoddle: I Was Mary Queen of Scots*. Here we proudly present some fascinating early entries from Sven's 2006 diary:

2 January

My old friend Tord Grip comes to call on me and asks if I am wishing to go and watch West Ham play Chelsea that afternoon. Sure, I say, but Nancy is not happy, claiming that I had promised to take her shopping in Bond Street. I put my foot down. 'Nancy!' I say. 'I am the England manager. I have to watch football matches. It is my job. You'll just have to find something else to do.' The matter is settled. We come back with five pairs of shoes and a silk scarf.

3 January

Get back from a meeting at the FA just in time to catch *Deal or No Deal* with Noel Edmonds. It is all about unscrupulous cash deals and people opening brown envelopes, and so offers excellent escapism from the world of football. It is my favourite show and for sure, I like Noel's style. I understand his wrinkly bottom used to be very popular once upon a time. I receive an invitation to go to Dubai next week for a football academy project. It sounds fun.

4 January

I assemble some of the England players for an informal get-together in Hertfordshire. I let them go off and enjoy themselves in the evening. Most of the squad go clubbing and chasing women, but Wayne Rooney chooses to visit an old people's home instead. How thoughtful. He is so misunderstood, that boy.

5 January

I tell Nancy I am off to do an interview with Garth Crooks. She thinks I said 'Garth Brooks' but I explain patiently, 'No, Nancy. This is not the multi-award winning, million-selling, international country-music artist, but rather a friend of Ray Stubbs.' Garth is in particularly fine form. He begins: 'Sven, now that England have once again qualified for the World Cup finals under your leadership, it is probably fair to say that, vis-à-vis the mordacious reaction after the Northern Ireland game, you are currently held in Brobdingnagian esteem thanks to the victory over Argentina, yet do you not feel that there is always a sense, in a case of déjà vu with previous incumbents of the post and bearing in mind that a prophet is invariably without honour in his own land, that your reputation could still be reduced to Lilliputian proportions, empires could crumble and mountains could come crashing into the sea if you persist with Owen Hargreaves as the holding player in midfield?'

7 January

I am pictured in the stand on *Match of the Day*. The BBC is legally obliged to show me on screen at whichever game I attend. It was an instruction from Nancy's lawyers, so that she knows where I am on a Saturday afternoon.

8 January

For sure, a boring day. There is never much in the Sunday papers. Off to Dubai in the evening. Remember to record *Deal or No Deal* and *Cash in the Attic*.

9 January

Dinner with the sheik in Dubai. Such a nice man. He is surprisingly interested in football and wants to know all about Wayne Rooney and how he deals with press intrusion. I tell the sheik:

Apparently Tord Grip loves the accordion; Sven's organ has also been much admired.

'He's just a poor boy from a poor family, spare him his life from this monstrosity.' We have champagne, crab cakes and lobster but, alas, there are no chocolate sprinklies for the ice-cream dessert. Buy Nancy some Immac in the duty-free shop at the airport.

11 January

Back home, I spend a quiet night in with Nancy. She wants to watch *Celebrity Big Brother* but I warn her that Faria Alam (or 'Wake-Up Alam' as she was known at the FA) is on it. So Nancy switches to Living TV, only to find Ulrika presenting a new show. Nancy is not happy. 'Isn't there anything on TV that I can watch without seeing one of your women?' she enquires. She is in a temper; I am in a half-nelson. Eventually we agree that *How Not to Decorate* with Colin and Justin should be safe viewing.

12 January

My faithful chum Tord Grip calls in for a coffee. I ask him to go to Ikea because Nancy wants some new shelves and I tell him to bring me the flat pack 4. He arrives at the house an hour later with Gary Neville, Rio Ferdinand, John Terry and Ashley Cole. I think poor Tord got the incorrect extremity of the stick.

14 January

I make sure I am shown settling into my seat at Highbury by the *Match of the Day* cameras, then I sneak out the back way and spend the rest of the afternoon in the local library, reading a book on ancient Roman ceramics. Arsenal win 7–0. Damn. I had them down for a draw.

15 January

I go for an early morning stroll in the park to feed the ducks. There is a black and white duck with whom I have established quite a rapport over the months, but this time my pleasure is short-lived because when I return home I somehow sense that maybe something is wrong. My suitcase is on the front step and a locksmith is changing the locks on the front door. Inside, Nancy is not happy. She hurls the Sunday papers at me, leaving quite a red mark on my forehead from the colour supplement and its free Barry Manilow CD, and screams that my picture is all over the front pages. 'I only met the woman twice,' I protest. 'It meant nothing.' But Nancy is still yelling about some fake sheik making a fool of me. Oh dear. For sure, I have been tricked. I decide to telephone the players mentioned in the article. I apologize to Wayne Rooney for saying he has a temper but he slams the phone down on me. I call David Beckham in Spain to clear up the Aston Villa misunderstanding but I get through to Victoria. She is not only angry at David being dragged into this but is also threatening legal action over the insinuation that she would ever consider setting foot in Birmingham. When I do speak to David, he says he has explained to Victoria that there are many similarities between Madrid and Birmingham. 'For a start,' he says, 'both have a Bull Ring.' Next I call Michael Owen's number but get through to a chat line by mistake. An hour later, a little breathlessly, I ring Rio Ferdinand to say that I am sorry for calling him lazy, but he is still in bed. Finally I manage to calm Nancy down. 'It is a lot of fuss about nothing,' I assure her. 'It will quickly blow over and will all be forgotten by tomorrow.'

HE SAID WHAT?

'No one. I fear nobody in the world, except my wife.'

Zambian coach Burkhard Ziese, when asked whom he feared in his country's qualifying group for the 1998 World Cup

16 January

Unable to get out of the front gate for photographers. Nancy unwittingly steps out into the spotlight and rushes back into the house in floods of tears – she has been photographed wearing the same red dress she wore for my last scandal!

18 January

I promise Nancy that, for sure, the press will soon get tired of this. We find a photographer in the laundry basket. Later I am summoned to the FA. They tell me to get a grip. I say I already have a grip – my trusty pal Tord Grip. Perhaps this is not the time for Swedish humour.

19 January

More press questions. The *Sun, Mail, Express, Times, Mirror* and *Telegraph* want to know if I intend resigning. *Heat* magazine wants to know my favourite vegetable. Because of all this, I miss *Deal or No Deal*.

20 January

Nancy is still not happy. I have a growing fear of waking up in bed next to a horse's head.

21 January

I go with my faithful sidekick Tord Grip to Burger King and ask for two whoppers. The man behind the counter says: 'You're going to lead us to victory in the World Cup and you never chase women.' I do not understand the English sometimes.

22 January

Nancy has cancelled the Sunday papers. I am furious with her – the second part of the Barry Manilow CD was in this week's issue.

23 January

After further revelations in the press, I am summoned once more to the FA. Brian Barwick is wearing his Liverpool scarf. That is

always a bad sign. I agree to the announcement that I am step-
ping down as England coach after the World Cup in Germany.
Nancy is not happy. She is threatening to telephone her brothers.

24 January

There is a lot of negative publicity about me in the newspapers
today. They love to rake up the past – about how I allegedly did
nothing at half-time during the 2002 World Cup defeat to Brazil.
That is simply not true. I had a very difficult crossword clue to
solve. It had been troubling me for days. Anyway, before the
players went out for the second half, I still found time to offer a
quick piece of advice to David Seaman: 'Be off your line quickly
to deal with Ronaldinho's free kicks.'

26 January

Nancy is prowling around the house like the bear with the sore
head. She is not happy that I am losing my job. We argue – that is,
she argues, I cower behind the sofa – for over an hour. She drags
up my little indiscretions once again and demands to know why
Ulrika always called me 'Svennis'. I tell her it was a rhyming nickname. This does not help. Two broken tea services later, she raises
the dreaded 'M' word. 'Why won't you marry me?' she screams.
'Why won't you commit?' For sure, she is wonderfully impressive
when she is angry and tonight she looks more ravishing than ever
as the light catches on the knife that is clenched between her
teeth. I manage to distract her momentarily with a Pronuptia
catalogue and make a dash for the front door. My dependable
comrade Tord Grip offers to put me up for the night.

27 January

Wearing my best buddy Tord Grip's old gardening clothes, I board
the plane for Montreux for the draw for Euro 2008. For the first
time in years I am uncertain what the future holds for me. I
wonder if Noel is thinking of moving on from *Deal or No Deal*?

DAYS OF MOURNING

COSTLY OWN GOAL

When Judith Chalmers was preparing her *Wish You Were Here?* city breaks in the early 1990s, it is safe to assume that the Colombian town of Medellin was not high on her list. As a tourist destination it left a lot to be desired, probably because the most common way of leaving Medellin was not in a plane but in a body bag. As the drugs capital of the world, Medellin had such a fearsome reputation that it made Johannesburg look like Frinton-on-Sea. When drunken Colombian youths talked about the crack in their arse on a Saturday night, they weren't speaking anatomically. Apart from drugs, Colombians' other great passion was football. All too often the pair went hand in hand as drug cartels and gambling syndicates tried to exercise their influence over the game. Thousands of pounds changed hands on the results of matches. Colombia was the only country where pools winners were presented with their cheques *before* the games had been played. And if things didn't go according to plan, someone would pay – usually with his life. In 1989 the Colombian League was suspended after referee Alvaro Ortega was assassinated.

The South American qualifying group for the 1994 World Cup saw tensions running typically high, and, in September 1993, when Colombia sensationally crushed Argentina 5–0 in Buenos Aires – Argentina's worst home defeat since 1910 – the people of Colombia took to the streets to celebrate. Twenty people were killed as the celebrations became too enthusiastic. When it was later claimed that the match had been fixed, nobody was exactly shocked by the suggestion, large-scale corruption being as much of an everyday occurrence in those parts as the TV weather forecast.

The ill-fated Colombian defender Andrés Escobar, shot dead after his own goal.

'I'm as baffled as Adam on Mother's Day.'

*Bolivia coach Xabier Azkargorta, dismayed that clubs
had refused to release players for his country's warm-up
games for the 1994 finals*

Even so, Colombia arrived in the United States unbeaten in
their six qualifying matches and with genuine hopes of lifting
the World Cup itself. They were many people's dark horses.
However, Colombia's preparations were accompanied by
persistent rumours that gamblers and drug barons were exer-
cising their influence over the squad. Coach Pato Maturana
had reportedly received death threats over matters of team
selection. Whatever the truth, Colombia's players looked edgy
and unfocused in their opening game against Romania at the
Pasadena Rose Bowl and slumped to a shock 3–1 defeat. Their
next opponents were the United States, a team they could
have been expected to beat comfortably. Instead the
Colombians strolled about as if it were a practice match. Even
the guy marking the lines had broken more sweat on the pitch.
After thirty-five minutes, Colombian defender Andrés Escobar
stretched to cut out a low cross, but merely succeeded in
diverting it into his own net. The Americans added a second
goal through Ernie Stewart and all Colombia could manage in
reply was a last-minute consolation. They were out of the
World Cup. Despite finally rousing themselves to beat
Switzerland 2–0 in their last group game, Colombia returned
home to a hostile reception. Escobar, whose own goal had
effectively put the team out of the competition, was philo-
sophical. 'This is football,' he said. 'Life goes on.' Tragically he
was only half right.

On 2 July – ten days after his unfortunate own goal – Escobar and his girlfriend were leaving a restaurant in a suburb of Medellin when they were confronted by a group of men. Following a brief altercation, one of the men snarled 'Thanks for the own goal' and pumped twelve bullets into Escobar, yelling 'Goal' each time he pulled the trigger. Escobar's murder shocked even hard-bitten Colombians. The next day, Alan Hansen remarked of another match at the finals: 'The Argentine defender wants shooting for a mistake like that.' The BBC issued a swift apology.

Speculation mounted as to whether the killer was just a disappointed fan or part of a more sinister plot. The reasons for the team's abysmal performances remained a mystery, although it was revealed that coach Maturana, who had resigned and gone into hiding, had withdrawn Gabriel Gómez from the line-up to face the United States after he too had received death threats. In June 1995, Humberto Muñoz Castro, bodyguard to a local millionaire, was convicted of Escobar's murder and sentenced to forty-three years in prison, although he was controversially released in 2005. It was claimed that he had acted on behalf of drug barons who had bet $20 million on Colombia defeating the United States.

Andrés Escobar was one of at least five professional footballers murdered in Colombia in the 1990s. And Sven thinks he has problems . . .

SHITE FACT

Ecuador's Colombian-born coach Hernán Gómez was shot in the leg during his country's qualifying campaign for the 2002 World Cup. His attacker was believed to have disagreed with the coach's team selection policy. Gómez subsequently resigned, but was persuaded to return to his post.

DEATH IN LAGOS

After losing 2–1 away to Gabon, Nigeria desperately needed to defeat visiting Angola to have any chance of reaching the 1990 World Cup finals. So it was that 100,000 people crammed into the 80,000-capacity Surulere Stadium in Lagos on the hot, dry Saturday of 12 August 1989. Every space in the stadium was taken four hours before kick-off. Among Nigeria's team was twenty-five-year-old Sam Okwaraji, a dreadlocked midfielder with a law degree and a devastating turn of pace. He spoke six languages fluently, which is six more than the average English player can muster, and was not afraid to stand up for his rights. Finding himself in the middle of a club-versus-country row, he stated that nothing would stop him playing for the national side. 'I am a Nigerian,' he stated proudly, 'and will die fighting for the dignity of my country.' Sadly, he did just that.

The game started badly for Okwaraji when, in the opening minutes, he received the first yellow card of his international career. With Nigeria hanging on to a 1–0 lead, things turned ugly when an Angolan player was sent off. As all eyes focused on the dismissed Angolan arguing with the referee, fate also handed Sam Okwaraji a red card. He suddenly slumped to the ground near the left touch-line and was quickly substituted. He was pronounced dead on arrival at hospital, having suffered a massive heart attack. It was a sad day all round for Nigerian football: in the crowd seven people were crushed to death, and although they won the game, Nigeria failed to reach the finals, pipped at the post by Cameroon.

SHITE FACT Before their victory over Hungary in the 1938 final, it was said that the Italian players had received a sinister telegram warning them 'Win or die.'

JOCK'S AWAY

The phrase 'firm but fair' is often a euphemism for 'bully', in much the same way that 'colourful character' is a euphemism for 'nutter' and 'Tomas Repka' is a euphemism for 'crap defender'. No doubt in his own mind Ivan the Terrible was firm but fair, but in Jock Stein's case the overused phrase was appropriate. Blunt, sturdily built and with little time for frivolity, he would have made a good Yorkshire farmer. Instead he was idolized by the Scots for his deeds with Celtic and respected throughout the world of football, a big man in every sense of the word. The autumn of 1985 saw Stein in charge of the Scottish national team as they strived for a place in the World Cup finals. On 10 September they travelled to Cardiff for the match that would decide their destiny: a draw would be sufficient to earn Scotland a play-off against Australia; defeat would give Wales a date with the Aussies.

Stein had not seemed himself that day. His assistant, Alex Ferguson, attributed it to a heavy cold. The tension in the Scottish camp was heightened when Mark Hughes put Wales ahead in the thirteenth minute and with Scotland goalkeeper Jim Leighton, who always bore the air of a badly assembled troll, flapping at everything, the outlook for the Tartan Army appeared bleak. Then, at half-time, Leighton explained his shaky display by revealing to his teammates that he normally wore contact lenses, but had lost one in the first half. Nobody had noticed any difference. Scotland were struggling to make any headway until, with twenty minutes remaining, Stein sensed that veteran Welsh fullback Joey Jones was tiring, and brought on tricky winger Davie Cooper. Ten minutes later Scotland finally made the breakthrough. They were awarded a soft penalty for handball and Cooper stroked the spot kick past Neville Southall. As the Scots counted down the last two minutes, the referee blew for a free kick but Stein, mistaking it for the final whistle, tried to clamber to his feet, sweat soaking his face. Suddenly he slumped against the team physio Hugh Allan, murmuring, 'I'm away, Hugh.' By the time the final whistle did go – and Scotland's passage was assured – team doctor Stewart Hillis was trying to save Stein's life in the medical room. At 9.50 p.m. he was pronounced dead from a heart attack. His last words being 'Doc, I'm feeling much better now.' Jock Stein didn't get much wrong in life, but this was an untimely and tragic exception.

SHITE FACT

Forced into a 1954 qualifying play-off with Turkey, Spain left out their star player László Kubala after receiving a threatening telegram. Without him Spain could only draw 2–2 and they went out of the tournament on the unlucky toss of a coin.

SICK AS A PARROT

TEARS OF A CLOWN

Until July 1990 there were only three scenarios where it was considered acceptable for a man to cry: the death of a close relative, the loss of a dearly beloved pet, or the failure of the last horse in a seven-race accumulator. But Paul Gascoigne changed all that. When Gazza burst into tears during the World Cup semi-final with West Germany, he showed that he was so in touch with his feminine side that they were practically dating. Suddenly men everywhere decided it was OK to cry in public, even if it was simply because someone had pinched their last Rolo.

Gazza had always possessed something of a fragile temperament, which, allied to an intellect that was only marginally superior to that of a plant, left him, as Bobby Robson generously put it, 'daft as a brush'. Hearing this comparison, brushes the world over were gravely offended and said to be consulting their lawyers. Put Gazza in the snarling, physical arena of a game of football and he was about as stable as a can of petrol in the presence of a lighted match, but this proud Geordie had his dream and that summer it was to appear in the final of Italia '90.

The prospect looked unlikely at first as England scraped through unimpressively from a tight group, drawing 1–1 with Ireland and 0–0 with Holland before edging a single-goal victory over Egypt. Wins against Belgium and Cameroon were equally hard-earned, but now England found themselves on the threshold of glory with only old foes West Germany barring their way to the final. Gazza had already picked up a yellow card against Belgium and then, early in extra time against the

Gazza was just grateful that the new-strength England shirt could accommodate a man-sized blow.

Germans, he launched into a senseless late tackle on Thomas Berthold and was rightly booked. Gazza may not have been the sharpest tool in the box – indeed he wouldn't have been the sharpest tool in a box full of blunt instruments – but he knew that two yellow cards in the tournament meant that he would miss the final if England got there. Suddenly the enormity of what he had done hit him. He thought of a World Cup final without him, and his lip began to quiver. Then he thought of a world without Mars bars, and he started blubbing uncontrollably. Gary Lineker famously gestured to the England bench, pointing to his eyes. This has variously been interpreted as 'Keep an eye on him', 'Have a word with him' or 'He's not right in the head'. 'Fetch him his dummy' might have been more appropriate.

Fortunately for Gazza's mental state, his Geordie buddy Chris Waddle was in the England line-up and when the tie went to a penalty shoot-out, the nation's hopes rested on Waddle's hunched shoulders. If you had to have someone take a penalty to save your life, Waddle would surely rank alongside Long John Silver. As he ran up to the ball, leaning back, his body was in the perfect position for taking a penalty . . . at rugby. Inevitably, he blazed the kick over the bar and England were out of the World Cup. All Gazza would miss was the third place play-off, a sporting event of barely greater significance than the Ludlow & District Tiddlywinks Final. And after losing 2–1 to Italy, the England team needed Gazza tears only to find their way back to the airport.

SHITE FACT

Héctor Castro, a key member of the Uruguay team that lifted the World Cup in 1930, had no left hand, having lost it in a childhood accident.

HE SAID WHAT?

'To be defeated by the United States at football was like the MCC being beaten by Germany at cricket.'

England captain Billy Wright

HORROR IN HORIZONTE

Back in 1950, England considered themselves to be the best team in the world even though, through their failure to compete in any of the previous World Cups, they didn't have the paperwork to prove it. They were able to call upon players of the calibre of Bert Williams, Alf Ramsey, Billy Wright, Tom Finney, Wilf Mannion and Stan Mortensen. Oh, and Stanley Matthews who, at thirty-five, could still tie a fullback in knots – that is, when England deigned to pick him. For Matthews divided the nation: half thought he was indispensable, the other half thought Finney was a better bet. Years later it was much the same story with Steve McManaman: half thought he was disappointing in an England shirt, the other half thought he was crap anyway.

Thus, with such talent to call upon, England travelled to Brazil for the 1950 tournament in high spirits. For their first game, FA chairman and sole selector Arthur Drewry omitted Matthews from the eleven, and was duly vindicated as the team beat Chile 2–0. Next up were the United States in Belo Horizonte. It was expected to be a formality against a bunch of American amateurs – whose line-up included a hearse driver, a teacher and a part-time dishwasher in a New York restaurant – rated at 500–1 to beat England by one London bookmaker. You could get shorter odds on Deputy Dawg becoming the next head of the FBI. In their warm-up games the US had lost

5–0 to Turkish club side Besiktas and 9–0 to Italy, and after losing 3–1 to Spain in their opening World Cup tie, they were so pessimistic about their chances that a number of their players went out partying the night before the game. With hindsight, perhaps England should have heeded the fact that the American camp contained two Scots – coach Bill Jeffrey and captain Eddie McIlvenny, the team's one professional, who had once played seven games for Wrexham before being given a free transfer. England kept roughly the same side that played Chile, which meant that once again there was no place for Stanley Matthews.

On a dry, bumpy pitch, England dominated from the outset, but were less successful than an Anne Diamond diet. Chance after chance went begging until eight minutes before half-time the restaurant dishwasher, Haitian-born Joe Gaetjens, glanced a header past Bert Williams. And despite England's increasingly frantic efforts, the United States somehow held on to that lead for the rest of the match. The 1–0 defeat came as such a shock that back home the English press thought the score was a misprint for 1–10. Meanwhile, with soccer of so little interest in the country, most American papers ignored the story completely while others thought the result was a hoax. England did have a chance to repair their damaged pride against Spain but, even with the recalled Matthews, they went down 1–0. As for the US, they also bowed out of the competition, crashing 5–2 to Chile, and so the goalscoring dishwasher never did get to lift the Cup.

SHITE FACT

For the 2006 World Cup a German firm has produced a cheese that looks like a football. The spherical smoked Gouda has a special black and white rind.

TOO COCKY

England were not the only country at the 1950 World Cup to fall victim to their own over-confidence. Host nation Brazil had cruised through to the final pool of matches, which, bizarrely, was going to decide the outcome of the tournament in the absence of an actual final. In their first game in the final pool, Brazil trounced Sweden 7–1 before putting six past Spain, during which Zizinho displayed a moment of breathtaking arrogance. After taking the ball round Spanish goalkeeper Ramallets, Zizinho waited for him to get up so that he could beat him again! It was like taunting a sick animal or waving a betting slip at Paul Merson. These two emphatic victories left Brazil needing just a draw from their last game – against Uruguay – to win the World Cup. And with Uruguay having been held 2–2 by Spain and only managing a 3–2 win over Sweden, Brazil were made overwhelming 1–10 favourites. The governor of the state of Rio even made a victory speech before the game, but it turned out that he wasn't just counting his chickens before they were hatched: he was doing a head count them before the cockerel had even arrived in town. Understandably peeved by his words, the Uruguayans resolved to make him eat them, and, after falling a goal behind early in the second half, they fought back to triumph 2–1. As the World Cup was being won in 1950, the only Englishman on the pitch was the referee, George Reader.

SHITE FACT

Brazil's homecoming victory parade following their triumph at the 2002 World Cup turned sour when fans in Rio threw rocks at the team's open-topped bus. The fans, who had been waiting for up to eleven hours, became violent on learning that the parade was being cut short because the players were tired.

HE SAID WHAT?

'We'll never lose a goal against an attack as weak as the Koreans. Maybe they will be a problem for other teams, but not for us.'

Polish defender Tomasz Waldoch before his team's 2–0 defeat to South Korea in 2002

WAS HE WORTH IT?

David Ginola. Gallic poseur or talented winger? Discuss.

Since football was originally conceived as a physical, manly game, there is a school of thought which says that players shouldn't do modelling. When David James did some work as a male model a few years back, there were concerns that he might think twice about diving at Alan Shearer's feet the following Saturday for fear of ruining his looks. Having said that, Shearer might have been equally worried in case having half of James's face stuck to his boot spoiled *his* boot sponsorship deal. Besides you never saw the likes of Tommy Smith or Ron Harris doing modelling, unless it was for machetes. As for hair products, while it was OK for former Sunderland and Manchester City winger Dennis Tueart to promote neat grooming, one-time Coventry City and Newcastle United hard man Brian 'Killer' Kilcline, who had enough hair to stuff several dozen cushions, wisely refrained from entering the world of advertising. Not so David Ginola. And to this day he is probably remembered less for his football and more for his flowing locks and the L'Oréal hair-product commercials in which he purred: 'Because I'm worth it.'

Unfortunately, by the time he'd branched out into the world of

To be dropped by France was bad enough, but to be accused of having split ends made Ginola's blood boil.

advertising, French football had long since decided that Ginola definitely *wasn't* worth it. He had always been considered something of a luxury player, but it was in the qualifying group for the 1994 World Cup that he really burned his bridges. With two games remaining – home fixtures against Israel and Bulgaria – France needed a single point to progress to the finals. They were apparently coasting against Israel until two goals in the final seven minutes gave the visitors an improbable 3–2 victory. No matter, there was still the Bulgaria game and with the score at 1–1 – and the match deep into injury time – the French fans were mentally booking their flights for the United States. Surely nothing could go wrong now. After all, France were in possession . . . with

Ginola. He could have done just about anything with the ball to use up the remaining few seconds but instead, in a flash of inspiration, he tried an ambitious pass that gifted possession to the Bulgarians. Moments later the ball was nestling in the back of the French net, courtesy of Emil Kostadinov. It was Bulgaria and not France that would be going to America. Ginola was never forgiven for his aberration and didn't feature in another World Cup tie. One wonders what his ''ealthy looking 'air' looked like after his teammates had run their studs through it.

SHITE FACT

Hosts Switzerland blamed their 7–5 defeat to Austria in the 1954 quarter-final on the unseasonably hot weather after it was revealed that their goalkeeper Eugene Parlier had been suffering from sunstroke.

DODGY WORLD CUP HAIRCUTS

Even Pierluigi Collina must have had a bad hair day once in his life. His 'wax and go' style is probably the neatest in modern football simply by default, because the days when players wore a grin as wide as their centre partings have been replaced by weird tonsorial creations that owe more to topiary than hairdressing. A cynic might suggest that some of today's players are so obsessed with keeping up appearances that they spend more time in the hairdresser's than on the training pitch. Over the past eight years David Beckham has had more different hairstyles than John Prescott has had free dinners. The latest craze is 'standout' hair. At the 1998 World Cup, Japan's Hidetoshi Nakata dyed his black hair red in the hope of catching the eye of European scouts. By the 2002 finals the Japan team sported seven vivid hair colours, from the bright crimson (once orange) of Kazuyuki Toda to the silver strands of Junichi Inamoto. And who could forget the Romanians at France '98? To celebrate reaching the second stage, the whole team, with the exception of the goalkeeper who was bald, bleached their hair. Dear old Jimmy Hill tried to persuade us that it was a cunning tactic to help the players pick out a teammate with a pass, but the bottle blondes could only draw with Tunisia before bowing out of the tournament to Croatia. Here are just about the ten worst World Cup haircuts of all time:

10. Colombian goalkeeper René Higuita sported a mass of black curls and ringlets that must have doubled his body weight.
9. Germany's Rudi Völler managed two crimes for the price of one – a mullet *and* a bad moustache. Sadly the style is still all the rage in Austria.

Meeting Colombia's Carlos Valderrama was truly a hair-raising experience.

8. Paul Breitner's Afro at the 1974 tournament. The German player inspired Kevin Keegan's perm. Say no more.

7. Nigerian defender Efe Sodje's 2002 chin lock – a single strand of beard jutting beneath his chin in the national colour of green. Apparently his wife spent hours working on the creation, though a pair of scissors could have saved her a lot of time and effort.

6. The Bobby Charlton comb-over from 1970. People say Beckham's hair changes with the wind, well Bobby's really did. Depending on the direction of the breeze, his hair would either flap across his bald pate or give the indication that he was turning left.

5. The David Seaman ponytail. Whereas Frenchman Emmanuel Petit could just about get away with the 'My Little Pony' look, it was truly ridiculous on a Yorkshireman. Its only saving grace was that it didn't look as daft as Harry Kewell's.

4. Others tried but nobody could match Chris Waddle's 1990 mullet. Perhaps if he'd worn it the wrong way round he might not have missed that penalty.

3. The green pigtails of Nigeria's Taribo West. They might be just about acceptable with a gingham dress in the school playground, but in the World Cup . . .

2. David Beckham's Mohawk left his head looking like a rough track where weeds had grown down the middle.

1. The World Cup's worst haircut has to belong to Carlos Valderrama, the Colombian who is usually described as looking as though he'd just been plugged into an electric socket. To others, his wild mane makes him the reincarnation of Lenny the Lion.

COACHING
CATASTROPHES

IF YOU CAN'T STAND THE HEAT . . .

Having upset the Mexican press with his customary brand of charm and tact, Sir Alf Ramsey knew that few tears would be shed locally if his team failed to retain the World Cup in 1970. The quarter-final draw had set England against West Germany in the ultimate grudge match. Ramsey's plans to overcome the Germans in the cauldron of León were dealt a severe blow on the eve of the game by the illness that hit Gordon Banks. While replacement Peter Bonetti was more than capable, he had not played competitive football for over a month. He was as rusty as an old sink and, on the day, about as agile. There was another bad omen when Lady Ramsey had gone to sit in her reserved seat in the stand, only to find it occupied by a Mexican who flatly refused to budge. She was not amused and returned to her hotel to watch the game on TV. She must have wished she had watched the Mexican version of *Crossroads* instead.

Yet it all began so promisingly with England easing into a 2–0 lead after fifty minutes, courtesy of goals from Alan Mullery and Martin Peters. In a last throw of the dice, the German manager Helmut Schoen sent on winger Jürgen Grabowski to exploit Terry Cooper, who was visibly wilting in the intense heat. Shortly after-wards Franz Beckenbauer strode forward elegantly and shot from outside the area. It looked innocuous enough until Bonetti help-fully dived over the ball. At 2–1, Ramsey, who was not known for making tactical substitutions, decided to replace Bobby Charlton and Peters with Colin Bell and Norman Hunter, perhaps with one eye on the semi-final. Although Bell was a fine player at club level, he was no Charlton, so it was like replacing a Rembrandt with a painting-by-numbers creation. With two of England's best players removed from the action, the Germans smelled English blood. First, with Bonetti stranded, Uwe Seeler looped a back header into the England net. Then, in extra time, Grabowski skinned the weary Cooper, and when his cross was headed back, Gerd Müller drove in the winner. Once again Bonetti was nowhere near the scene of the crime.

Much of the blame for England's defeat was laid at Ramsey's door. His substitutions changed the course of the game – but not in the manner he had intended. He was never again held in such high esteem by the English public or indeed by his employers, and four years later he was sacked when England failed to qualify for the 1974 World Cup. As for the Germans, they had gained partial compensation for defeat in the 1966 final. And soon they would unleash their ultimate revenge on the English people: it was called Blue Nun.

SHITE FACT

As Brazil struggled through their early matches at the 1978 finals, irate supporters took to the streets of Mar del Plata and burned an effigy of manager Cláudio Coutinho.

FIT FOR ACTION?

The 1998 World Cup final was expected to be a showcase for the talents of Ronaldo, the twenty-one-year-old Brazilian striker who was hailed at the time as the world's greatest player. But the real Ronaldo failed to show up in the Stade de France that evening, replaced instead by an impostor who would have looked out of his depth in Unibond League Division One. The circumstances surrounding Ronaldo's lacklustre display have since been shrouded in sufficient mystery to exercise the mind of Miss Marple, and while nobody knows for certain what happened in the build-up to the game, he was clearly not in a fit state to wear the Brazil shirt. It is believed that early on the afternoon of the final, Ronaldo suffered some kind of convulsion in his hotel room. He was rushed to hospital but doctors could find nothing wrong. Coach Mario Zagallo initially left him off the original team sheet, and then changed his mind. Zagallo later refuted allegations that the team's sponsors Nike had demanded that Ronaldo play.

It was clear from the start against France that Ronaldo was a shadow of his normal self. He looked as out of place as Arsène Wenger in a lap-dancing club yet Zagallo refused to substitute him. After France cruised to a 3–0 win, the Brazilian coach was left to defend his decision. Even Zagallo's dismissal three weeks later failed to halt the speculation: had Ronaldo been physically unfit or had he simply succumbed to the pressure associated with being the nation's saviour? Happily the real Ronaldo showed up for the 2002 final – scoring both goals against Germany – but his current club form with Real Madrid casts doubt as to which version will be on display in the 2006 finals. Still, at twenty-nine, time is on his side. Nobody could say he's long in the tooth.

SHITE FACT

A month after the 1998 World Cup final, Mario Zagallo took legal action to force Brazilian star Romário to remove a huge caricature of the former national coach from the toilet door of a bar he owned.

HE SAID WHAT?

'We couldn't lose and yet we lost. The whole thing was unreal, a freak of nature.'

Sir Alf Ramsey on the 1970 defeat to West Germany

WE'RE ON THE MARCH WITH ALLY'S ARMY

When it comes to great Scottish comic figures, you tend to think of Billy Connolly or Rab C. Nesbitt. Yet if you were born south of the border, there's none that can compare with Ally MacLeod. The best thing to have come out of Scotland since the A74, MacLeod was a truly inspired comic creation in the Frank Spencer mould. He had the comedy nose, the hangdog expression, a hilarious way with words, and his timing was exquisite. Who else would be crazy enough to predict that Scotland were going to win the World Cup shortly before their humiliating campaign in Argentina? It wasn't as if Scotland's history in the tournament exactly inspired confidence. True, they had talented individual players – particularly in midfield – but could MacLeod succeed where others had failed by moulding them into a team? From the moment of qualification, MacLeod decided to make increasingly rash statements in the hope of deflecting pressure from the players. With uncharacteristic foresight, he said, 'If things go wrong, everybody's going to blame me. I have been the big mouth and I will take the rap.' Nobody could dispute the 'big mouth' bit. At the time the only thing around with a comparable sized mouth was being hunted by Roy Scheider on the movie screen.

MacLeod's thirst for publicity remained unquenched. 'I'm a winner,' he declared, failing to recognize that guiding Ayr United

Ally MacLeod: the face that launched a thousand quips.

to runners-up spot in the Scottish Second Division was not quite the same as lifting the World Cup. Since he and his players were now convinced that the World Cup was theirs for the taking, nobody bothered much with preparation out in Argentina. Peru were thought to be easy pickings, so Scotland's subsequent defeat almost left MacLeod lost for words. Things got worse – the Willie Johnston affair, the embarrassing draw with no-hopers Iran – leaving MacLeod a forlorn figure, ridiculed in two hemispheres. Famously, he concluded a press conference by patting the head of a stray dog and saying, 'You, my old son, may be the only friend I have left in the world.' The dog promptly bit him on the hand. Rumour has it that a Scottish Rolling Stones fan went to his rescue and told the dog, 'Hey, you, get off MacLeod.'

In all fairness, Ally MacLeod had never been particularly lucky. On his playing debut – for Third Lanark in November 1949 – the Cathkin Park stand had caught fire, forcing the players to grab their kit as four fire engines turned up to douse the blaze, and in the summer of 1978 it looked as though his world was going up in smoke again. Despite a battling, but ultimately futile, 3–2 victory over Holland, Scotland returned home to widespread derision. As the blame game intensified, MacLeod resigned and returned to the less troubled waters of club management.

SHITE FACT

As a player Daniel Passarella was renowned for his flowing locks, but when he was appointed coach of the Argentine national team following the 1994 World Cup, he immediately announced that he would not be picking any players with long hair.

HE SAID WHAT?

'I don't even know where these bloody places are on the map.'

Jack Charlton after Ireland were grouped with Latvia and Lithuania in qualifying for the 1994 World Cup

GRUDGE OVER TROUBLED WATER

Whereas some managers give the impression of knowing a great deal when they actually know very little, Jack Charlton tended to adopt the opposite approach. He sometimes cultivated the image of a bluff buffoon better acquainted with fishing than international football. As Republic of Ireland manager, legend has it that he didn't always know the names of his own players, let alone the opposition. But anyone who underestimated him did so at their peril. For like the unemployed jester, he was nobody's fool. His playing nickname of 'The Giraffe' was equally misleading. Giraffes are silent, peaceful creatures whereas Charlton always had plenty to say for himself and claimed to have kept a 'little black book' of opponents due for retribution, which suggested that it was safer to cross the Mafia. So his nickname was no more appropriate than calling Bobby Charlton 'Shaggy' or Norman Hunter 'The Gentle Giant'.

After leading Ireland in their heroic quest at Italia '90, Charlton repeated the feat four years later. With no British teams qualifying for the 1994 finals, we immediately adopted the Irish as our own, and took to drinking Guinness, wearing green shirts and, of course, two condoms – to be sure, to be sure. This may have seemed opportunistic but, to be fair, we were no less Irish than the team's players, who hailed from such far-flung corners of the Emerald Isle as Glasgow, Liverpool and Lambeth.

Once in the USA, the Irish got the party off to the best possible start by despatching Italy with a Ray Houghton goal. Their second opponents were Mexico in the heat of Orlando. Understandably the Mexicans handled the conditions far better and tempers were becoming heated on the Irish bench. Concerned for his players' welfare, Charlton wanted to make sure they took in plenty of water during the match, but in doing so he fell foul of certain FIFA guidelines that seemed to be made up on the spot. And when, with Ireland trailing 2–0, he tried to bring on John Aldridge, the match officials delayed the substitution to such an extent that there was a very real danger Aldridge wouldn't get on until France '98. After an angry altercation with the linesman, Aldridge was finally allowed to join the action in time to score Ireland's consolation goal. Charlton was subsequently fined some $15,000 and banned from the bench for the next game. Aldridge was fined nearly $2,000. Feeling he was paying the price for his protests over the water breaks, Charlton growled, 'Next time we'll play Mexico in winter and see what happens.'

A dreary goalless draw with Norway was enough to put Ireland into the second round but there another improbable adventure ended as the Irish crashed out of the competition to Holland by two goals to nil. British allegiance was immediately withdrawn. Having raised the level of expectation, Charlton wasn't sure what sort of reaction he would receive from the fans back in Ireland, but mused, 'I suppose I'll only know how they feel when I return on Thursday and if I have to pay for my own Guinness.'

SHITE FACT

The master plan of South Korea coach Cha Bum-Kun against Holland at France '98 was to leave his best players out of the starting line-up and then bring them on as a secret weapon during the game. It was a bum decision. Korea lost 5–0 and Cha was sacked.

DID HE NOT LIKE THAT!

There are three sentences that should strike fear into any England manager: 'Take me over your desk, big boy, next to the photo of the Swedish national team', 'I'm an Arab sheik, and I want to be your friend' and 'I'd like to make a sympathetic television documentary about your job.' It was Graham Taylor's misfortune to fall victim to the third of these when he unwisely agreed to take part in the infamous Channel Four documentary *An Impossible Job*, chronicling England's attempts to qualify for the 1994 World Cup. Having failed to reach the finals of the 1992 European Championships and been likened to a root vegetable in *The Sun*, Taylor could not have been on shakier ground had he been straddling the San Andreas fault. Whereas his predecessors – and indeed his successors – were able to choose from the full à la carte England menu featuring some world-class players, it was unfortunate for Taylor that due to injury, retirement and loss of form, he was forced to make do with the lunchtime set menu, which contained such unpalatable dishes as Carlton Palmer, Lee Dixon and David Bardsley. As for Andy Sinton, we'd have been better off with Dale Winton; at least he would have stiffened up the back four. And when you rely on Nigel Clough – a player with the top speed of a mobility scooter – to inject a little pace into the side, you know you're in trouble. So Taylor should have kicked the documentary offer into touch, for it turned out to be as painful to watch as *Celebrity Fit Club . . . On Ice*.

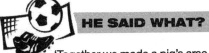

HE SAID WHAT?

'Together we made a pig's arse of the situation in Norway.'

Graham Taylor on England's 2–0 beating in Oslo in June 1993

'I said, "That's a turn-up." I didn't call you a turnip. Honestly.'

England's qualifying bid went off the rails in the summer of 1993 when a fortuitous 1–1 draw in Poland was followed by an abject display in Norway resulting in a 2–0 defeat. Taylor's tactics were as baffling as his decision to select Des Walker, who had even forgotten how to play from memory. A controversial 2–0 defeat in Holland all but sealed England's fate and even though they whipped little San Marino 7–1 in their final game – despite falling a goal behind in eight seconds – the game was up and Taylor resigned six days later.

When the documentary aired, it was like watching a man drown. As events conspired against him on the field of play, Taylor was heard resorting to his favourite phrase 'Do I not like that!' If only he'd chosen 'Nice to see you . . . to see you nice,' he might have got away with it. Alongside him, assistant Phil Neal was Little Sir Echo. Matters came to a head in Holland when Ronald Koeman, who should have been sent off for a cynical professional foul on David Platt minutes earlier, put the Dutch ahead with a disputed free kick. Taylor was understandably angry with German referee Karl-Josef Assenmacher and snapped at the linesman, 'Tell your friend out there that he's just got me the sack.' The TV documentary ensured Taylor remains haunted by his catchphrase to this day. What a pity he'd never had the opportunity to use the infinitely preferable 'Good game . . . good game.'

SHITE FACT

Costa Rica employed no fewer than five different managers during their successful qualification for the 1990 World Cup.

141

NOBBY STILES AND OTHER ANIMALS

THE BATTLE OF BORDEAUX

When Brazil met Czechoslovakia in a second-round match at the 1938 World Cup in France, it ended up like a scene from *Casualty*. The final score was one broken leg, one broken arm, one serious stomach injury, two lesser injuries, and three sendings-off. Two Brazilians – Zezé Procopio and Arthur Machado – were sent off by the Hungarian referee Paul Hertz along with Czechoslovakia's Jan Riha. The skilful Oldrich Nejedly sustained a broken leg and his Czech teammate, goalkeeper Frantisek Planicka, was forced to play on with a broken arm. A third Czech, Josef Kostalek, suffered the stomach injury. The match finished 1–1, necessitating a replay two days later.

FIFA might have been excused for ordering extra bandages and stretchers for the replay, but in the event it passed off peacefully, largely because so many of the combatants from the first game were unable to take part. Without their injured stars, the Czechs lost 2–1. Brazil had been so certain of victory that their main party left for Marseilles – where the semi-final against Italy was due to take place – even before the replay had kicked off. Ultimately, however, overconfidence was to prove the Brazilians' downfall as coach Ademar Pimenta crazily elected to rest his leading goalscorer, Leônidas da Silva, for the semi-final. It was the equivalent of George Martin deciding to rest Paul McCartney from the recording of 'Hey Jude'. In Leônidas's absence, Brazil slumped to a 2–1 defeat and had to settle for third place in the competition, achieved via a 4–2 victory over Sweden in which the recalled star scored twice to bring his tournament total to eight. Not surprisingly, Senhor Pimenta had one or two questions to answer when the team returned home.

SHITE FACT

The 1934 quarter-final between Spain and Italy was so violent that for the replay the following day seven Spaniards and three Italians – including one with a broken leg – were ruled out through injury.

THE BEAST OF SEVILLE

It takes a special talent to beat Hitler into second place in a survey to find the world's most hated man. Particularly when the person in question has neither been responsible for anyone's death nor probably given a second thought to achieving world domination. But German goalkeeper Harald 'Toni' Schumacher managed the unwanted feat in a French newspaper poll following his outrageous challenge on France's Patrick Battiston at the 1982 World Cup. It was without doubt the worst tackle in the entire history of the tournament, a premeditated collision reminiscent of another German Schumacher, and all the more inexcusable for the fact that it apparently warranted neither apology nor punishment.

The setting was the semi-final in Seville, a clash between French flair and German efficiency. The last time France really had a team to shout about, the Eiffel Tower was still just a blueprint, but now, with a side built around the extravagant talents of Michel Platini, there was hope – among neutrals as well as the French themselves – that they would have too much artistry for those perennial party-poopers, the Germans. Platini used to perfect free kicks in training by curling the ball around a line of life-sized, rigid wooden dummies, which was thought to be good practice for facing the Germans. For the first hour there was little to choose between the teams. Then, with the score at 1–1, Battiston, who had only just come on as a substitute, ran on to a sublime through ball from Platini. Anticipating the danger, the

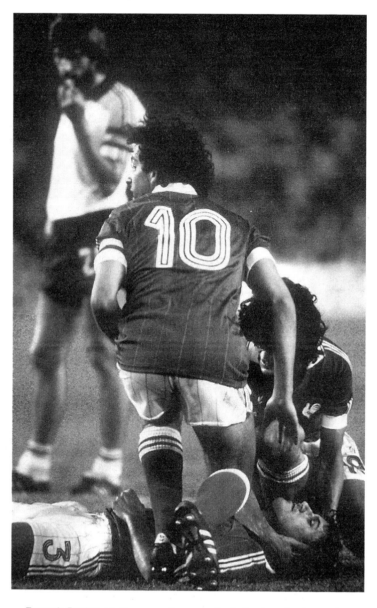

France's Battiston is the worse for wear after being brutally clattered by German keeper Schumacher in 1982.

burly figure of Schumacher came charging out of his penalty area, wild-eyed, arms flailing. Unnerved by this raging bull, Battiston could only poke the ball wide of the gaping goal, but the absence of the ball was immaterial as far as Schumacher was concerned. His sole objective was to ensure that Battiston did not get past him and so, without any thought of applying the brakes, he clattered into the Frenchman, brutally knocking him to the ground with a forearm smash of such force that it broke Battiston's jaw and knocked out two of his teeth. While Battiston lay motionless on the ground amid fears that he had suffered a fatal injury, Schumacher showed absolutely no interest in his condition. Equally reprehensibly, Dutch referee Charles Corver saw no infringement of the rules and simply awarded West Germany a goal kick.

The unconscious Battiston was given oxygen in the dressing room and spent a number of weeks in hospital. Schumacher was barracked for the rest of the match, and in extra time it looked as if justice would be done when the French moved into a 3–1 lead. But while they may have lacked grace on this occasion, the Germans rarely lack spirit and they fought back to level matters, sending the tie into a penalty shoot-out. And with no sense of shame, Schumacher, the man who should not have been on the pitch, pulled off two saves to send West Germany through to their fourth World Cup final. France were left with the consolation of being everybody's favourite losers. Inevitably, Schumacher protested his innocence, arguing that he was no more than careless. Little Bo Peep was careless; Harald Schumacher was guilty of a far graver crime. And the scariest thing is, compared to Oliver Kahn, Schumacher's a pussycat.

SHITE FACT

French defender Laurent Blanc used to kiss the bald pate of goalkeeper Fabien Barthez for good luck before each of his country's games at France '98.

ARTHUR'S TOUGHEST CHALLENGE

Even as a referee on TV's *Jeux Sans Frontières*, Arthur Ellis was a stickler for the rules. Barely a week would go by without him informing Stuart Hall that he'd had to disqualify someone. They all came the same to Arthur. It didn't matter whether it was an inflatable Belgian penguin, a Swiss milkmaid in a wetsuit, or the daughter of Clacton's lady mayoress wearing a giant beachball: if they'd broken the rules, Arthur would disqualify them without fear or favour. In his gaily striped jacket, whistle permanently poised near his lips, Arthur resembled an officious holiday-camp entertainments officer on the lookout for infringements in the knobbly-knees contest, but for many years he had been one of Britain's foremost football referees. And at the 1954 World Cup in Switzerland, he was called upon to control a match that required every ounce of his disciplinary zeal.

The quarter-final between Hungary and Brazil on 27 June 1954 has become known as 'The Battle of Berne'. A year after their historic 6–3 win at Wembley, the 'Magnificent Magyars', as they had been christened, were the favourites to lift the World Cup, but Brazil provided formidable opposition at the unfortunately named Wankdorf Stadium. Two goals down inside seven minutes, Brazil adopted an increasingly physical approach to thwart the Hungarians as the match became more niggly and petulant than Prime Minister's Question Time. With Arthur Ellis's whistle working overtime, the teams traded penalties before Brazil pulled it back to 3–2 with twenty-five minutes left on the clock. Five minutes later, Brazil's Nilton Santos and Hungary's József Bozsik began brawling after Bozsik reacted angrily to the Brazilian's challenge. Arthur had no hesitation in sending the pair off and when Brazil's trainer marched on to argue about the decision, he was also ejected. As the match threatened to develop into a full-scale bloodbath, Djalma Santos was seen chasing Zoltán Czibor around the pitch. In the closing minutes, Czibor exacted revenge by laying on the goal that sealed Hungary's 4–2 victory, but there was still time for Brazil's Humberto Tozzi to be dismissed for a nasty foul. A tearful Tozzi sank to his knees to plead for mercy, but Arthur remained unmoved.

There was more to come. At the final whistle, Ferenc Puskás, who had missed the game through injury, reportedly struck Brazil's Pinheiro in the face with a bottle. The furious Brazilians reacted by storming Hungary's dressing room and in the mayhem several Hungarian players were said to have had their faces slashed. Pinheiro subsequently left the ground with a bandage wrapped around a five-inch head wound, but amazingly neither side was punished over the disgraceful scenes. Given his way, Arthur, still seething after Hungary's centre half Gyula Lorant had laughed in his face when he booked him, would almost certainly have disqualified both teams – even if Hungary were playing their joker.

SHITE FACT

Uruguay's José Batista was sent off after just fifty-five seconds of the 1986 group match with Scotland. Uruguay, who had already had a player sent off against Denmark, were threatened with expulsion from the tournament unless they cleaned up their act.

LICENSED TO KILL

Nobby Stiles was never an obvious choice to play James Bond. With his lack of front teeth (he looked more like 'The Man With The Golden Gum'), short, stocky frame and eyesight worse than Mr Magoo, he would surely only have landed the part of 007 if the Elephant Man were unavailable. Yet Stiles was Alf Ramsey's secret agent in England's quest to win the 1966 World Cup, an unsung hero licensed to kick the crap out of the opposition. Stiles's attributes were not immediately apparent. As a midfield player he was a poor passer of the ball and an infrequent goalscorer. Even teammate Jack Charlton conceded that, 'When it came to the more artistic side of the game, Norbert was not the

Nobby Stiles ruffled more feathers than a fox in a henhouse.

HE SAID WHAT?

Alf Ramsey to Nobby Stiles: 'Put Eusebio out of the game.'

Stiles to Ramsey: 'For tonight or for ever?'

kind of bloke to stand out in a crowd.' He was a Happy Eater next to Bobby Moore's Savoy Grill, but what he lacked in finesse, Stiles made up for in determination and an ability to man-mark the most dangerous of players. He was like a rabid Jack Russell, forever snapping at the heels of the opposition. Certain members of the FA would willingly have had him put down.

During England's final group match with France in 1966, Stiles scythed down Jacques Simon directly in front of Wembley's Royal Box. Afterwards, two FA chiefs, who were worried that a sensitive soul like Prince Philip might be offended by such blatant aggression, demanded that Ramsey drop Stiles for the next game, to which the England manager replied that he would resign if Stiles didn't play. Naturally, Stiles remained in the team, and later in the semi-finals carried out his duties to perfection in stifling Portugal's Eusebio. And as England paraded the World Cup, it is the image of Nobby Stiles's toothless grin and little jig – like a garden gnome on Ecstasy – that has lived longest in the memory.

SHITE FACT

As he went up to collect the World Cup, Bobby Moore noticed that the Queen was wearing white gloves. Fortunately he had the presence of mind to wipe his muddy hands on his England shirt before shaking hands with Her Majesty.

A SPOT OF ARGIE BARGY

At first glance it was an unequal contest: a small, bald, insignifi-cant-looking man against a tall, dark, athletic figure with the looks of Dean Martin and the attitude of Dirty Harry. German referee Rudolf Kreitlein versus Argentina captain Antonio Rattín. But in this instance it was the little guy who wielded the power, who had the metaphorical gun in his pocket. And he definitely wasn't pleased to see Rattín.

The 1966 quarter-final between England and Argentina was fraught from the outset, with the officious Herr Kreitlein dashing around with an autograph hunter's enthusiasm for collecting names. And each Argentine booking was always fiercely contested by their spokesman Rattín, who loomed menacingly over the little German. Rattín was trying to run the game but Kreitlein was having none of it. The battle of wills continued when Rattín himself was cautioned for a relatively innocuous foul on Bobby Charlton – innocuous in that it didn't involve spitting or hair-pulling. And let's face it, Bobby Charlton's hair could sometimes have been pulled from ten yards away. Then, nine minutes before half-time, the referee booked another Argentine, Luis Artime. Inevitably, Rattín disputed the decision, but this time Herr Kreitlein snapped, rather like Captain Mainwaring at the end of his tether with Private Pike. To Rattín's astonishment, the referee pointed to the dressing room. The Argentine captain had become the first player to be sent off at Wembley for eighteen years – except that Rattín had no intention of leaving the field. For eight long minutes he and his teammates argued with the referee. The entire Argentine team appeared on the verge of walking off until Rattín was finally persuaded to go, slowly, reluctantly, leaving the pitch to a chorus of jeers, boos and cries of 'Get off'. It was like being at a Jim Davidson show.

After England's 1–0 victory (by virtue of a Geoff Hurst goal), an incensed Alf Ramsey physically prevented George Cohen from swapping shirts with any opponent. Later, Ramsey famously described the Argentine players as 'animals', carefully choosing to ignore the presence of Nobby Stiles in his own line-up or the fact that in the course of the match England committed nearly twice as many fouls as Argentina. Ramsey believed he held the moral high ground. Besides, they were only foreigners.

SHITE FACT

When the final whistle sounded in Oslo to confirm Norway's shock 2–1 victory over England in a 1981 qualifying tie, Norwegian radio commentator Bjorge Lillelien lost the plot. In a state of excitement verging on the hysterical, he invoked such names as Lord Nelson, Sir Winston Churchill, Clement Attlee, Henry Cooper, Lady Diana and Margaret Thatcher, before adding triumphantly, 'Can you hear me, Maggie Thatcher? . . . Your boys took a hell of a beating!' His bizarre commentary has kept Denis Norden and others in work for twenty-five years and was parodied in a newspaper in 2005 when England's cricket team captured the Ashes from Australia: 'Kylie Minogue! Steve Irwin! Holly Valance! Crocodile Dundee! Natalie Imbruglia! Ian Thorpe! Mrs Mangel! Can you hear me? Your boys took one hell of a beating!'

ONE NIGHT IN ISTANBUL

European football supporters tend to enjoy a trip to Turkey as much as George W. Bush and Tony Blair would enjoy a night on the town in Baghdad. For Turkish grounds are the sweaty armpits of Europe – they're unpleasant, hairy, and nobody wants to go there. So it was with some trepidation that Switzerland prepared for the second leg of their World Cup play-off in Istanbul in November 2005. The Swiss had a two-goal cushion from the first leg, but they knew that they would need to show enough bottle to match those that would be thrown at them from the stands. And although Switzerland lost 4–2 on the night, they went through on the away-goals rule – a result that sparked the inevitable hail of missiles from the crowd at the final whistle. The Swiss players ran for the apparent safety of the tunnel, but one of them, Valon Behrami, appeared to be deliberately tripped by Turkey's assistant coach Mehmet Özdilek, who in turn received a retaliatory kick from behind by Behrami's teammate Benjamin Huggel. Players from both sides – including Alpay, a serial offender in football terms – then became involved in an ugly brawl, which required the intervention of security staff, one of whom was taken to hospital. Joining him there was Swiss defender Stéphane Grichting, an unused substitute who needed treatment after being kicked in the groin during the fracas. According to a teammate, Grichting had been attacked by the local police who vowed, 'We're going to slit your throat!' The Turkish police argued that this merely constitutes helping them with their enquiries. FIFA president Sepp Blatter, who just happens to be Swiss, threatened draconian measures against the Turks, including the possibility of banning them from the 2010 World Cup. In the end, Turkey were ordered to play their next six competitive matches abroad and behind closed doors, which greatly reduces their chances of qualifying for the 2008 European Championships . . . in Switzerland.

SHITE FACT

At the end of Switzerland's 2–1 victory over Italy in 1954, Brazilian referee Mario Viana was chased around the pitch by angry Italian players.

HE SAID WHAT?

'There's only one team going to win it now, and that's England.'

Kevin Keegan, two minutes before Dan Petrescu's winner for Romania at the 1998 World Cup

SHOWDOWN IN SANTIAGO

To say there was no love lost between Chile and Italy in 1962 is like saying that José Mourinho and Arsène Wenger/Sir Alex Ferguson/Frank Rijkaard/Bryan Robson are not exactly bosom buddies. South American countries had long been angered by the Italians stealing their best players and the tense situation was heightened at the start of the World Cup when a couple of Italian newspapers published derogatory articles about host nation Chile. One journalist wrote to the effect that Chilean women were ugly slappers. This was not calculated to foster a spirit of goodwill between the two countries. So when Chile and Italy met in a first-round match in Santiago, FIFA were expecting all hell to break loose, apart, of course, from the bit of hell that is forever Luton.

Just as Arthur Ellis found himself in charge of the 'Battle of Berne' in 1954, so another English referee, Ken Aston, officiated at what became known as the 'Battle of Santiago'. The match was barely eight minutes old before Aston was obliged to start reducing the numbers. Reacting badly to a tackle from behind, Italy's Giorgio Ferrini kicked out at Chile's Landa. Aston sent Ferrini off, but the Italian refused to go and the match was delayed for ten minutes until a combination of Italian officials and armed police managed to escort him from the pitch. Then Chile winger Leonel Sánchez, the son of a professional boxer, broke the nose of Humberto Maschio in an off-the-ball incident.

The linesman, standing a few feet away, somehow failed to spot the offence. He should have gone to Specsavers.

Early in the second half, Italian defender Mario David decided to take revenge on Sanchez by kicking him in the head. Unfortunately for the Italians it showed up on Aston's radar, and he duly sent David for an early bath. Down to nine men, the Italians eventually succumbed 2–0. And the players couldn't even drown their sorrows that night by picking up a few local girls. For after what had been written in the press, they would have been safer taking their chances with a firing squad than with any Chilean women.

SHITE FACT

There were sixty-nine free kicks in Argentina's 1–0 defeat of Bulgaria at the 1962 tournament. One Bulgarian player even had stud marks down his spine.

AN A-Z OF THE WORLD CUP

Amnesia – Antigua's 1994 World Cup qualifier in the Netherlands Antilles was delayed for eighty minutes because the hosts had forgotten to provide the Antiguan team with transport from their hotel.

Bayonets – Soldiers with fixed bayonets patrolled the Centenario Stadium in Montevideo during the 1930 final between Uruguay and Argentina. Fans were searched for firearms, the Argentine players received a mounted police escort, and Belgian referee Jean Langenus only agreed to officiate hours before kick-off after securing a guarantee of safety for himself and his two linesmen.

Crime – With echoes of Bobby Moore's unfortunate brush with the law in Colombia, Senegal midfielder Khalilou Fadiga was accused of stealing a gold necklace from a shop in Daegu, South Korea, during the 2002 finals. Fadiga, who insisted it was just a practical joke, returned the necklace and the store manager decided not to press charges, even sending Fadiga a small gold pig, a good-luck token in South Korea.

Drugs – In 1974, Haiti's Ernest Jean-Joseph became the first player to be sent home from the World Cup for failing a drug test.

Execution – Alex Villaplane, who captained France in their first ever World Cup match in 1930, was shot by the Resistance fourteen years later on suspicion of collaborating with the Nazis during the Second World War.

Frankenstein – A 1934 qualifier between Hungary and Bulgaria was refereed by Herr Frankenstein of Austria.

Gambling – Desperate for money, an Albanian man gambled his wife on the result of the Argentina–Bulgaria group match at the 1994 finals, which the Bulgarians surprisingly won 2–0. He then complained to the police when his wife left him for the winner of the bet.

Home bias – Haiti qualified for the 1974 finals thanks to a 2–1 victory over unlucky visitors Trinidad and Tobago, who had no fewer than four goals disallowed during the match.

Incompetence – Having arranged the 1950 tournament on a league basis, the organizers completely forgot about scheduling a final. Luckily for them, the last match in the competition – between Brazil and Uruguay – determined the destiny of the trophy and has therefore assumed the status of a World Cup final.

Jobsworth – The England–Uruguay game that opened the 1966 finals was almost called off after Hungarian referee Istvan Zsolt discovered that seven of the England players had left their identity cards at the team hotel. Zsolt maintained that the game could not go ahead unless the cards were produced and so a police motorcyclist was quickly sent to fetch them.

Killing – A man in the Thai capital of Bangkok shot his wife dead in a row over the 2002 World Cup. He was watching a match when she snatched the remote control and switched to a soap opera.

Looting – In March 2005, an angry mob of Mali fans set fire to cars, looted shops and caused damage to monuments in Bamako after earlier storming the pitch and forcing the abandonment of a qualifier against visitors Togo. Police fired tear gas to quell the rioters following a late winner by Togo. The match was later awarded to Togo.

Misunderstanding – While Brazilian players were lining up a free kick 30 yards from goal in 1974, Zaire's Ilunga Mwepu inexplicably rushed from the defensive wall and booted the ball upfield. He was booked for his trouble.

Nobbled – On the night before England's 1970 quarter-final with West Germany, the world's number-one goalkeeper Gordon Banks mysteriously went down with a bout of poisoning after drinking a bottle of beer, prompting suspicion that his drink may have been spiked. Peter Bonetti was called up as his replacement. The rest we know.

Oooops! – Having been allowed to keep the Jules Rimet Trophy after winning it for a third time, Brazil contrived to lose it in 1983. It was stolen from its home in Rio and has not been seen since.

Prison – A group of seventeen prisoners escaped from a Brazilian jail in 2002 while the nation was glued to the country's opening World Cup match against Turkey. They timed their breakout through a tunnel to coincide with kick-off, knowing that the guards would be distracted.

Qualification chaos – Wales were originally eliminated from the 1958 qualifiers by Czechoslovakia, but earned a reprieve courtesy of the Middle East conflict. Although Israel and Egypt had been at war since 1955, FIFA, in a stroke of genius, put Israel into the Africa/Asia qualifying group whereupon Egypt, Sudan, Turkey and Indonesia withdrew rather than play them. This left Israel with a bye to the finals, but since this was contrary to recently introduced FIFA regulations, it was decided to draw lots among the group runners-up to see who would meet Israel in a play-off. Wales were pulled out of the hat and by beating Israel 2–0 both home and away, they qualified for the finals for the only time in their history . . . albeit as representatives of Africa and Asia!

Rubbish – After finishing bottom of their group in the 1958 finals, Argentina were pelted with rubbish on their return home.

Sex – Spanish players were accused of accessing porn sites in the run-up to the 2002 finals. The Spanish coach, José Antonio Camacho, had attempted to repair a frosty relationship with the press by inviting them to the team hotel in South Korea. But one journalist – from an Argentine paper – found his way into the hotel's cyber café and discovered that the players had been logging on to a site called Strip Players, which offers to bring 'private strippers live to your desk-top'.

Tragedy – Five years after finding the World Cup, canine hero Pickles was killed after being strangled with his own lead while he was chasing a cat up a tree.

Urinating – When a stray dog ran on to the pitch and disrupted England's 1962 quarter-final with Brazil in Chile, it was Jimmy Greaves who apprehended the pesky mutt. The disgruntled dog had the last word, however, when he peed all over the England player – presumably to avenge his capture.

Video nasty – West Germany's victory over Holland at the 1990 finals was marred by the sendings-off of Holland's Frank Rijkaard and Germany's Rudi Völler. Television replays clearly showed Rijkaard spitting twice at Völler.

Rudi Völler was unfortunate to find himself within spitting distance of Frank Rijkaard.

Witch doctor – Before Australia met Rhodesia in a play-off in November 1969, their players accepted a Mozambique witch doctor's offer to curse the Rhodesians by planting bones near the goalposts. Australia won the match 3–1, but their amateur players couldn't afford the witch doctor's £1,000 fee, so the curse was apparently placed on them instead. Three Australian players were mysteriously taken sick before their next game.

X-rated – During a qualifying match in April 2001, a terrible tackle by Trinidad and Tobago's Ansil Elcock left Mexico's Cuauhtémoc Blanco with a bad knee injury. In the days that followed, the foul was shown repeatedly on Mexican television and aroused such hostility that Trinidad coach René Simões deliberately left Elcock out of the return game in Mexico.

Yelling – Following Hungary's shock defeat in the 1954 final, irate fans yelled abuse at the team on their return to Budapest, and smashed the windows of manager Gustav Sebes' house.

Zzzzzz . . . – When the opening match of the 1974 finals – between Brazil and Yugoslavia – ended 0–0, it was the third successive World Cup in which the opening game had finished goalless.

All Michael O'Mara titles are available by post from:

Bookpost, PO Box 29, Douglas, Isle of Man, IM99 1BQ

Credit cards accepted.
Telephone: 01624 677237
Fax: 01624 670923
Email: bookshop@enterprise.net
Internet: www.bookpost.co.uk

Free postage and packing in the UK.

Other Michael O'Mara humour and sports titles:

Shite's Unoriginal Miscellany – 1-84317-064-7 hb £9.99

Eats, Shites & Leaves – 1-84317-098-1 hb £9.99

A Shite History of Nearly Everything – 1-84317-138-4 hb £9.99

Shitedoku – 1-84317-182-1 pb £3.99

You Are What You Shite – 1-84317-166-X hb £6.99

Crap Teams – 1-84317-111-2 hb £9.99

The World's Stupidest Sporting Screw-Ups – 1-84317-039-6
     pb £4.99

England: The Football Facts – 1-84317-188-0 pb £12.99